CODEPENDENCY CONFUSION

RECOVERY DISCOVERY

CODEPENDENCY CONFUSION

Developing Healthy Relationships

Randy Reynolds & David Lynn

ZondervanPublishingHouse
Grand Rapids, Michigan
A Division of HarperCollins*Publishers*

Codependency Confusion
Copyright © 1992 by Randy Reynolds and David Lynn

Requests for information should be addressed to:
Zondervan Publishing House
Grand Rapids, Michigan 49530

ISBN 0-310-57361-0

All Scripture quotations, unless otherwise noted, are taken from the HOLY BIBLE: NEW INTERNATIONAL VERSION® (North American Edition). Copyright © 1973, 1978, 1984, by the International Bible Society. Used by permission of Zondervan Publishing House.

"NIV" and "New International Version" are registered in the United States Patent and Trademark Office by the International Bible Society.

All rights reserved. No part of this publication may be reproduced, stored in a retrieval system, or transmitted in any form or by any means—electronic, mechanical, photocopy, recording, or any other—except for brief quotations in printed reviews, without the prior permission of the publisher.

Edited by Linda Vanderzalm
Cover design by Lecy Design
Cover photo by Dan Hummel
Interior designed by Ann Cherryman

Printed in the United States of America

92 93 94 95 96 97 / DP / 10 9 8 7 6 5 4 3 2 1

CONTENTS

	Acknowledgments	6
	Introduction	7
1.	The Victim: Learn to Take Responsibility	11
2.	The Rescuer: Let Go of Responsibility	18
3.	The Caretaker: Learn to Give *and* Receive	27
4.	The Overreactor: Give Up Anxiety	35
5.	The Controller: Give Up Dominance	43
6.	Dealing with Guilt	51
7.	Setting Boundaries	58
8.	Negotiating Contracts	65
9.	Breaking the Pattern: Intervention	74
10.	Finding Love in Healthy Ways	82
	Leader's Guide (Purpose, Format, Ground Rules, Group Process, Referrals, Qualifications for Group Leaders)	91
	Suggested Readings	96

To all the participants in the codependency groups sponsored by Renewal Counseling Ministries; and to our wives, Lynn and Kathy, for their patience and encouragement

Acknowledgments

We would like to express our deep appreciation to each of the following people:

Becky DeVoe, who typed, edited, and gave practical suggestions.

Sandy Kline, who led several codependency groups for Renewal Counseling Ministries, helped with the Bible studies, and gave practical suggestions in the writing of this book.

A special thanks to Vickie Pyland, who along with Dana Wilcox led the first codependency group, for all her enthusiasm and promotion.

Thanks to all the leaders of the codependency groups: Dr. John and Janice Williams, Betty Seery, and Linda Ross.

Introduction

Codependency can be a confusing term. Let's see if we can clarify it for you. A codependency is an unhealthy relationship that develops when one person in the relationship is very needy or dependent and the other person allows those needs to dictate the terms of the relationship.

The emotionally needy person in the relationship may be a spouse, a child or parent, a friend, or a co-worker. The need may express itself in mild behavior patterns like unrealistic expectations and unhealthy dependence or in more severe patterns of depression, compulsive behavior, addictions, alcoholism, eating disorders, or verbal or sexual abuse.

The codependent is the person who *allows* these needs to dictate the dynamics of the relationship. An adult man who allows his mother's overprotectiveness to determine where he goes on vacation is a codependent of his mother's emotional needs. A woman who allows her employer's perfectionism to dictate how many extra hours she spends at her job, away from her family responsibilities, is a codependent. A husband whose alcoholic wife's behavior determines how he relates to their friends is a codependent of her needs.

Codependency can take on various forms and roles. Some codependents respond to the needs of others by taking on the roles of helpless victim, rescuer, or caretaker. Other codependents respond by trying to control the needy person. Still other codependents respond by compromising ideals and behaviors they shouldn't compromise. Nearly all codependents struggle with insecurity, guilt, and confusion.

This confusion is especially acute for the Christian. The man may realize his mother's overprotectiveness is dominating his life decisions, but when he decides to do something about it, he may think, *Doesn't the Bible ask us to "bear with one another in love"? Should I stand my ground with my mother or bear with her?* The woman may realize that she must choose the needs of her family over her employer's demanding perfectionism, but she may think, *Doesn't the Bible tell us to go the extra mile for the other person? Am I being selfish in saying no to my boss?* The man may realize that he has to stop lying to cover up his wife's drunkenness, but he may wonder, *Doesn't the Bible say that love is patient and endures all things? What should I do?*

Our goal in this book is to help you work through issues involved in codependent relationships. But most important, we hope this book helps you make progress toward a Christian understanding of codependency. The people in the three examples are right. The Bible does tell us to bear with one another in love, go the extra mile, and love each other patiently. But the issue in codependent relationships is *balance*. When does bearing with someone injure both you and the other person? When does going the extra mile for one person's unhealthy needs endanger your God-given responsibility to other people? When does patience and endurance only further a behavior pattern that is destructive both to you and the other person?

At first glance, some of the advice given to codependents seems contrary to what we think of as Christian behavior. "Take care of yourself" and "Set boundaries" seem to be selfish responses, products of a "look-out-for-Number-One" mentality. Yet codependents need to hear this advice. Their relationships are out of balance, broken. And in order for wholeness to be restored, codependents may need to counterbalance their behavior with responses that would be out of line for interdependent relationships.

Finding the biblical balance will not be easy. And for that reason we recommend that codependents work through their issues with a group of Christians who can help them determine how to change and find wholeness.

The codependency movement can be dangerous for Christians. Because many treatments for codependency were developed without reference to Scripture or Christ, the counsel is often individualistic, emphasizing self-love, self-interest, and self-rule. This perspective overlooks the value of relationships with God and others.

One couple, who was suffering from marital and money problems, was nearly destroyed by such counsel. When they came to a therapist—who was affiliated with a church but trained in secular codependency counseling—he labeled them both as codependents and said they were too dependent to live together. He suggested they split up and learn to "take care of themselves." The couple separated, placing tremendous strain on the woman, who had custody of their two small children and needed to work outside the home to support the three of them. The physical separation didn't help them to achieve emotional independence and personal responsibility. Six months later, both husband and wife were still angry, critical, fearful, and focused on each other's wrongs.

The danger in much secular psychology is that the emphasis is so strongly on the health of the individual that it may lead to neglect of

God or others. However, extreme "Christian" counseling that ignores personal needs is equally dangerous.

This book will try to show you how to take care of yourself without compromising or violating your responsibility to God and other people. It will try to eliminate the rigid thinking that says, "I either love others and God, or I am selfish and love myself." Scripture provides a more balanced view. At times it will permit you to protect yourself, as in Matthew 7:6, "Do not give dogs what is sacred; do not throw your pearls to pigs. If you do, they may trample them under their feet, and then turn and tear you to pieces." Other times Christ puts the issue differently, "But I tell you who hear me: Love your enemies, do good to those who hate you, bless those who curse you, pray for those who mistreat you. If someone strikes you on one cheek, turn to him the other also. If someone takes your cloak, do not stop him from taking your tunic" (Luke 6:27–29).

Christ says that you need to be *both* self-protective and self-sacrificing. You can be loyal to yourself, God, and others. One loyalty doesn't exclude the others. Taking care of another person and overlooking personal needs may be necessary at times, like the parent who sacrifices sleep to take care of an infant. At another time setting boundaries and protecting yourself may be the necessary response, like telling a friend you won't lend her any more money until she takes responsibility for her finances and gets a job.

The Serenity Prayer contains two elements that can bring freedom to your codependent behavior. The first phrase, "God, grant me the serenity to accept the things I cannot change," expresses the need to accept or surrender your responsibility to control or change other people's behavior, like a spouse's alcoholism, work compulsion, or financial irresponsibility. A tremendous peace of mind comes from not feeling responsible to change others. The second element, "the courage to change the things I can," puts the focus back on you personally, because only you with God's help can change your behavior patterns, attitudes, and passivity. This second element is often the most important and most difficult because many Christians are afraid that developing more independence and self-sufficiency goes against their marriage, family, or God. A Christian can be both competent and dependent on God.

HOW TO USE THIS WORKBOOK

This Recovery Discovery workbook will explore the various roles codependents take on: the helpless victim, the rescuer who tries to fix everyone else's life, the caretaker who plays the martyr and does all the giving, the overreactor who sees all of life as a crisis, the controller who dominates other people's lives. Several chapters help you work through strategies for developing positive patterns: how to set healthy boundaries, how to negotiate a contract, how to find love in healthy ways, how to build interdependent relationships.

Each chapter consists of six sections. *Recovery Focus* highlights the issues the chapter will discuss. *Recovery Information* not only explains the issues but also discusses the confusing aspects of the particular issue for Christians. *Recovery Stories* are case studies that describe codependent behavior in various life situations. Questions following each story help you analyze the codependent behavior, furthering your understanding of the behavior patterns as you see them in the stories as well as in your own life. *Recovery Probers* are questions that help you take a personal look at your own codependent behavior. The *Recovery Guide* is designed to help you explore Scripture passages that will bring that needed balance in both your understanding and your life. At the end of each chapter, *Recovery Goals* help you formulate goals that you can work on to further your recovery from codependency.

Take the time to write out your answers to the questions in each chapter. Reflect carefully on your feelings and beliefs. Pray, asking God to use this workbook as a tool to bring balance back into your life. Then discuss your insights and feelings with someone—ideally with a small group that will study this workbook together.

If you are part of such a group, speak up. Share your thoughts with the group. Look to the others for help and support. Learn from them as they share their stories and struggles. Pray together, depending on God to work in your life. And rejoice together as you grow and find wholeness in your recovery from codependency.

If you aren't able to be part of a small group, talk over your recovery process with a trusted pastor, counselor, or balanced friend. Share your responses and questions with that other person. Ask him or her to pray for you regularly.

1. The Victim: Learn to Take Responsibility

RECOVERY FOCUS

- Break the passive-dependent pattern that keeps you codependent.
- Learn to take responsibility for your own life and decisions.
- Become independent without losing your identity or love for others.

RECOVERY INFORMATION

Do you see yourself as a helpless victim of circumstances or relationships that have trapped you? Do you see yourself as overly dependent on other people and their thoughts of you? Do you gain most of your sense of self-esteem, security, and identity from your relationships to other people?

LOOK IN THE MIRROR

Read the following characteristics and check those that describe you:

- [ ] I am a victim of injustice, dominance, or abuse.
- [ ] I lack self-esteem.
- [ ] I use helplessness to gain alliances.
- [ ] I lack confidence in my thoughts, feelings, and desires.
- [ ] I am not assertive.
- [ ] I adapt myself to other people.
- [ ] I appear weak to other people.
- [ ] I feel fearful.
- [ ] I feel helpless.

☐ I feel depressed.

☐ I feel afraid of abandonment.

☐ I feel resentful.

☐ I feel powerless.

☐ I feel hopeless.

CODEPENDENCY CONFUSION

What does a Christian do in this situation? Does a Christian passively accept everything that happens as "God's will"? Does a Christian have the right to "take control" of a situation?

This chapter will help you examine the various dynamics of your codependent role and help you to move beyond passive dependence. It will explore case studies and Scripture passages that give perspective on the confusion many Christians feel about this codependent role and help you to trust in God and to establish healthy interdependence with other people.

God desires to give you personal power instead of a groveling and helpless dependence. "For God did not give us a spirit of timidity, but a spirit of power, of love and of self-discipline" (2 Tim. 1:7). A healthy relationship to God will empower you to work toward emotional interdependence.

RECOVERY STORIES

#1 FARMER FRUSTRATION

There once was a young farmer who planted a crop every spring in a fertile valley he inherited from his father. Everything went fine until a herd of wild horses settled in the area and began to destroy the farmer's crops. He complained to nearly everyone about the horses. "All I have is this little valley, and the horses have trampled and eaten my crops. They are ruining my life."

Out of fear and desperation, the young farmer traveled to the village to talk to the resident wise man. When he found the wise old man, the young farmer blurted out his story. He concluded by helplessly mumbling, "I have been cursed because I live in the valley where the wild horses run, and I can't control them."

The old man looked up at the farmer and said, "Are you sure these horses are a curse? Are you sure you can do nothing to change your situation? You are not a helpless victim."

"What do you mean?" responded the farmer, with surprise in his voice.

"Did your father give you that valley for you to serve it or so that it would serve you?" retorted the wise old man.

"I never asked myself that question," said the farmer. "I guess the valley is meant to serve me," he said thoughtfully.

"Then," said the sage, "your task is to decide how it will serve you. You have many options."

"Options? I don't know what you are talking about. I see my only option as living with this curse," said the farmer.

The wise man looked him straight in the eyes and said, "Think about it. If you own the land, then you have control over how you use it. Do you have to use it to raise crops? What are your options?"

The young man thought for a minute, and the lights went on in his head. "Yes, I see what you're saying. I don't *have* to be a farmer, just because my father was a farmer. As you suggested, maybe this 'curse' is really a blessing in disguise. I'm going to go home and think about my options. You're right. I can do something about my situation."

The young farmer went away empowered. Soon he became master of a valley full of domesticated horses, which he sold throughout the countryside. He became so competent at raising horses that people came from miles around to learn his secret.

1. **What were the young farmer's beliefs *before* recovery?**
   a. I can't change anything.
   b. I'm a victim, and I must passively suffer.
   c. I'm dependent on the circumstances, things, and people around me. They can affect me, but I'm helpless to affect them or myself.

2. **What were his changed beliefs *in* recovery?**
   a. I have options!
   b. The wise old man enabled me to have the courage to change the things I could change.
   c. I need to take responsibility for several areas of my life. I must not just depend on others or I will be victimized.

3. **What were the farmer's dominant feelings *before* recovery?**
   a. Helplessness
   b. Hopelessness
   c. Resentment

4. What were his changed feelings *in* recovery?
   a. Confidence
   b. Hopefulness
   c. Power to change his life

5. What were the farmer's behavior patterns *before* recovery?
   a. Complaining
   b. Withdrawing
   c. No initiative

6. What were his changed behavior patterns *in* recovery?
   a. Acting creatively
   b. Recognizing his options
   c. Gaining control of the horses

#2 DOWN BUT NOT OUT

Betty came to counseling after a series of bad relationships. Her first husband, who was abusive both physically and verbally, had left her for another woman. Suddenly she found herself alone in New York City with two small children and no marketable skills. Desperate, she grabbed onto the first man she could find, only to discover several years later that he was molesting her daughter. She was afraid to confront him, so she left him and began to live with an alcoholic man.

Finally, at age thirty-six, she came in for counseling. First she began to work on her personal growth: she began to read her Bible, and she started taking classes at a local community college. Her success at school and the support of her church gave her the courage to move out of the alcoholic's house and live on her own.

In her younger years, Betty had felt that without a man she would be nothing. She was terrified of being alone. But through counseling she learned that she had to face her fears in order to grow and be capable of a healthy relationship. Therefore, although several men were interested in her, she decided to wait until she accomplished some of her personal goals before she became involved in a serious relationship.

1. What were Betty's beliefs *before* recovery?

2. What were her changed beliefs *in* recovery?

3. What were Betty's dominant feelings *before* recovery?

4. What were her changed feelings *in* recovery?

5. What were Betty's behavior patterns *before* recovery?

6. What were her changed behavior patterns *in* recovery?

7. How are you like Betty?

RECOVERY PROBERS

1. In what situations do you see yourself as a victim?

2. How have these beliefs affected your behavior?

3. What new beliefs will you need for recovery?

4. What feelings contribute to your victim behavior?

5. How have you allowed these feelings to control you?

6. What new feelings will you want *in* recovery?

7. What behavior patterns keep you in a victim role?

8. What new behavior patterns will help you take charge of your life?

9. When will you take the first step to implement this new behavior?

RECOVERY GUIDE

When we depend on circumstances or relationships to give us security, self-esteem, or identity, we are disappointed. People and circumstances let us down, and we end up feeling like helpless victims. The Bible offers two important perspectives. We should depend, first of all, on God for our value, self-esteem, and security. Second, we can act in God's power to take responsibility for our situation. Instead of feeling that we can't do anything ourselves, that we can't take care of ourselves, that we'll fail if we try something new or different, we can trust God to help us make necessary changes.

Read Isaiah 31:1.

1. In what relationships do you need to depend less on the other person and more on God?

2. How can you express your dependence on God?

3. In what specific ways can Christ help you be less dependent on others and take more responsibility in your relationships?

Read Joshua 1:1–9.

1. Will God ever leave you alone? What does that mean to you?

2. How does God empower you to fight life's battles?

3. How do you gain strength and courage?

4. What can you do in order not to give in to the fear and discouragement that surrounds you?

RECOVERY GOALS

1. What "victim" issue do you need to address?

2. In what relationships do you need to develop a more healthy and godly independence?

3. How will your life be different if you have victory over this issue?

4. What steps can you take to move out of your victim role?

5. How will you develop more courage?

6. How can you take charge of areas in which you are now passive?

2. The Rescuer: Let Go of Responsibility

RECOVERY FOCUS

- Move from responsibility *for* others to responsibility *to* them.
- Let go of your need to fix people's lives, trusting God to lead them.
- Learn to accept the people you can't change.

RECOVERY INFORMATION

Maybe you don't see yourself as a helpless victim who needs to learn responsibility but as a person who is burdened by taking on *too much* responsibility for other people. You spend your life feeling responsible for the lives of your children, spouse, parents, friends, or neighbors. You often are frustrated that you can't change or fix their lives.

What's hard about this role is that you are always dissatisfied with other people and you rarely experience peace of mind. You may even find that in taking care of everybody else, you've neglected your own needs. You may not enjoy your own life because you are so overinvolved and frustrated with other people.

Growing out of this codependent role involves moving from feeling *responsible for* others, to being *responsible to* them; it involves moving from frustration with other people to an acceptance of who they are. It involves trusting God and letting go. It involves accepting the part of the Serenity Prayer that says, "God, grant me the serenity to accept the things [people] I cannot change."

CODEPENDENCY CONFUSION

The confusion in this area of recovery arises from this question: As Christians, are you responsible for other people? Yes—and no. We are told to "bear one another's burdens," but we are also told that "each of us will give an account of himself to God" (Rom. 14:12).

The important element in solving this dilemma is understanding what *responsibility* means. Yes, you are responsible to help other people, but you are not responsible *for* them. If a spouse or friend makes a poor choice, you are not responsible for that choice; you are not accountable for that choice. The friend or spouse is personally accountable to God.

In different relationships being *responsible to* takes on different definitions. Being responsible to a child as a parent is different from being responsible to a spouse as a spouse. You need to think through your different relationships and be clear where you need to be *responsible for* or *responsible to*.

Responsible for means	*Responsible to* means
1. I get my self-esteem mainly from how others are doing.	1. I get my self-esteem mainly from how I'm doing and from God.
2. They can't do it without me.	2. I allow others to do it themselves or leave them alone to learn.
3. I protect them from the natural consequences in their lives.	3. I allow them to learn from the consequences of their behavior.
4. I can control other people's behavior.	4. I admit my limitations and trust God for results in other people.
5. I don't listen; I give solutions and answers—and I'm right!	5. I supportively listen but also am genuine about my feelings, beliefs, values, and standards.
6. I rescue other people, ignoring my own needs and feelings.	6. I do my part in taking care of a spouse, parent, or friend, but I also take care of myself.

Responsible for means	*Responsible to* means
7. I get critical and blame others when they don't measure up to my expectations.	7. I focus on what I'm responsible to do, not what others aren't doing according to my desires.
8. I'm cold or harsh without acknowledging how it affects others, because I feel justified in doing so.	8. I'm honest and genuine, and I work on being kind and loving, because I'm accountable to God for my behavior.
9. I focus more on changing others than I do on changing myself. I feel powerless, but I don't turn this over to God.	9. I work on myself first and allow God to change me. I feel empowered in my life.

Another aspect of the confusion about Christian responsibility is knowing what to do when a person's refusal to take responsibility affects you. Are you, then, responsible for that person? How do you accept someone who is doing something wrong? "Accept one another, then, just as Christ accepted you, in order to bring praise to God" (Rom. 15:7).

When people refuse to take responsibility, it's not your responsibility to *make them* take responsibility. You may tell them how their irresponsibility affects you. You may be honest and genuine with your feelings and still love them. You may accept them and dislike their behavior patterns.

If they don't change, you can tell them how you are going to respond. Joan was afraid of driving with Ron, her husband, because he would lose his temper in traffic and drive recklessly. Joan told Ron how much it frightened her when he got angry, went over the speed limit, and made erratic lane changes. Ron responded by saying, "Tough. What do you expect with all those other crazy drivers?" Joan informed him that she wouldn't be driving with him anymore because it frightened her too much. She set a limit on how much she was willing to endure.

Just as each snowflake is unique from all others, people also vary in their personalities, perspectives, backgrounds, values, feelings, and desires. Learn to celebrate this diversity rather than be frustrated by it.

Learn to accept each different person as a part of God's diversity in creation.

Sarah and Linda were very different. Sarah and her husband had seven children and were involved in a close-knit church that saw children as a woman's mark of validation from God. Linda, married to an older man who didn't want children, had a satisfying career teaching young children in school and was involved in a church that valued women with professional careers. Sarah felt very frustrated with Linda and felt sure that if only Linda would become a mother, their friendship would be more pleasant and Linda would be much happier. Sarah felt it was her job to straighten Linda out by getting her off birth control and getting her to have children. Their relationship suffered for years, and they finally stopped seeing each other.

Sarah's unhealthy sense of responsibility and her inability to accept differences led to a destroyed relationship. Sarah needed to learn to accept Linda as she was, not try to make her a clone of herself. And Sarah needed to allow Linda to be responsible for her own decisions.

RECOVERY STORIES
#1 GET A LIFE

For years after Joe's wife died of cancer, he put his life on hold, postponing career moves or any other major decisions. He said, "I know I need to move on with my life, but I'm afraid. Maybe I wouldn't make it in this next career move. I'm afraid of working with new people. I'm afraid of starting over again; my wife was such a help to me."

To distract himself from his own pain, Joe became inordinately involved in his daughter's life. Elise, twenty-four years old at the time, kept getting involved with unstable men. When Joe would nag her about her choices of men, she would accuse him of being controlling and critical. "I worry about you every day, Elise. I only want to help you find stability. I want you to have a good job and a husband and a family."

When his relationship with his daughter became unbearably strained, Joe finally went for counseling help. The counselor helped him focus on his own life and find the courage to take responsibility for his decisions. He made a career move that gave him tremendous satisfaction.

By taking responsibility for himself, he was able to disengage from Elise's life and spend less of his energy trying to take responsibility for her decisions and future. He was finally able to tell her, "I'm sorry for trying to run your life. It's really your choice who you date and what you do with your career. I've been worrying about you, but I'm surrendering that to God. I believe you can make wise choices. I still may not approve of your choices, but I'll work on not being critical." That was the beginning of a renewed closeness between Joe and his daughter. They both had their ups and downs and adjustments to make in the next year, but they saw continued improvement in their lives and relationship.

1. **What were Joe's beliefs *before* recovery?**
   a. Gaining security from my daughter is more important than attending to my own issues.
   b. If I don't worry about and control my daughter, she won't do well.
   c. Trusting God with other people's lives won't help.

2. **What were his changed beliefs *in* recovery?**
   a. If I do what I'm supposed to do and face my pain and fear, it will help others as well.
   b. God and Elise are responsible for her life, and I can let go of control.
   c. God cares for my daughter, and he will help her.

3. **What were Joe's dominant feelings *before* recovery?**
   a. Anxiety about Elise's life
   b. Frustration about Elise's choices
   c. Anxiety about unresolved personal issues

4. **What were his changed feelings *in* recovery?**
   a. Freedom and relief from worry over Elise—serenity
   b. Courage and determination to confront personal changes
   c. Warmth and affection toward Elise

5. **What were Joe's behavior patterns *before* recovery?**
   a. Invading Elise's life and trying to control it
   b. Arguing, lecturing, and criticizing Elise
   c. Refusing to make career moves and personal changes for fear of failure

6. **What were his changed behavior patterns *in* recovery?**
   a. Communicating acceptance to Elise and releasing her to be responsible for her own life

b. Working on encouraging Elise through communication and refusing to argue or be engaged in a power struggle
   c. Making choices to walk through personal fears and do something constructive about them

#2 BE LIKE ME

Be-Like-Me, a huge man with massive limbs, was one of the greatest knights of the realm. He was revered by all the people of the country because he had fought many battles and had saved his village countless times from marauding bands of thieves.

Be-Like-Me had a son named I-Wish-I-Could, a lovable little guy, and I do mean little! He could barely lift—much less wield—his father's sword when he was fourteen. Be-Like-Me tried everything to teach his son battle skills. I-Wish-I-Could just wasn't built for it and really didn't have the temperament for it. His father was continually frustrated with him and couldn't see any of I-Wish-I-Could's gifts and talents: his relaxed way with people, his intelligence, or his creativity.

When I-Wish-I-Could reached manhood, his father decided to take him to another country to fight in a battle. They traveled for many days to join the hundreds of knights of the city called Diversity. However, Be-Like-Me and his fellow warriors were losing the battle because they were fighting giants who were larger and more organized than they were.

The leaders of Diversity called all the knights to a meeting to talk about a battle plan. Be-Like-Me was invited, and he brought along I-Wish-I-Could. The meeting soon turned into bedlam, with each knight bragging about his prowess and past successes. Power struggles broke out, and nothing was accomplished.

Just as the meeting was about to break up in frustration, I-Wish-I-Could spoke up. "I know how we could unify and conquer," he said boldly.

Be-Like-Me was totally embarrassed and felt his son was out of line because he wasn't an experienced warrior. "Be quiet," he told I-Wish-I-Could.

A wise old knight spoke up, saying, "I want to hear the boy's ideas." I-Wish-I-Could began to lay out a battle plan using the strengths of each knight who had spoken of past victories. His plan was so brilliant that the men gladly embraced it. Diversity, now unified, went out and conquered the giants.

I-Wish-I-Could became a hero, not because he was a brave fighter but because he listened well and thought clearly. His name was changed to I-Can-and-I-Did. His father was overjoyed and never again complained of the boy's size. I-Can-and-I-Did gained a greater reputation than his father's, even though he still couldn't lift his dad's sword. Be-Like-Me said to his son, "From now on I'll be called Be-Yourself."

1. What were Be-Like-Me's beliefs *before* recovery?

2. What were his changed beliefs *in* recovery?

3. What were Be-Like-Me's dominant feelings *before* recovery?

4. What were his changed feelings *in* recovery?

5. What were Be-Like-Me's behavior patterns *before* recovery?

6. What were his changed behavior patterns *in* recovery?

7. How are you like Be-Like-Me?

RECOVERY PROBERS

1. In what relationships do you need to let go of your unhealthy sense of responsibility?

2. What areas of control or responsibility do you need to let go?

3. How can you let go and still show that you care?

4. How can you take care of yourself without controlling other people?

5. What are the weaknesses of your personal strengths?

6. What are your spouse's (children's, parents', friends') strengths? What are the weaknesses of these strengths? How can you capitalize on the parts you enjoy? How can you release yourself from the parts that frustrate you?

7. What areas do you still feel responsible *for?* How would that be different if you were just responsible *to?*

8. How can you show acceptance?

RECOVERY GUIDE
Read Romans 14:1–12.

In this situation the people who did not eat meat sacrificed to idols were worried about the spirituality of those believers who did eat meat sacrificed to idols, and vice versa. And those who kept certain religious holidays criticized those who did not keep the holiday. Each group felt superior and critical toward the other group.

1. Were the people who did not eat meat sacrificed to idols responsible for those who did? What were they to do with their concerns?

2. How does God give freedom in this passage? How are believers encouraged to give others freedom?

3. How do you give others freedom to be accountable to God and not to you?

Read Romans 14:17–19.
1. What does *edification* mean? How do you facilitate edification in your relationships?

2. What are the goals of kingdom relationships? How do you experience joy with those with whom you disagree?

RECOVERY GOALS

1. What person do you have a difficult time accepting? Why?

2. Do you need to change? How?

3. How are you investing in this relationship? How do you need to invest in it?

4. When will you give up your frustration?

5. How do you keep yourself frustrated and lose your serenity? Will you quit doing that? When?

3. The Caretaker: Learn to Give *and* Receive

RECOVERY FOCUS

- Move toward reciprocity in relationships.
- Recognize and articulate your needs.
- Accept others' gestures of giving to you.

RECOVERY INFORMATION

Another area that needs to be brought into balance in the lives of codependents is the dynamic of giving and receiving. You may feel that you are always the one who gives, always the one to take care of things, while others seemingly just take and demand more. You think to yourself, *Why do I always have to be the one to give? Doesn't it occur to anybody that I have needs too? It sure would be nice if someone just for once took care of me.* And the resentment builds.

The balance comes in learning to develop reciprocating relationships—relationships in which both people give and receive. Sociologists say mutual giving is what balances all social systems. This is especially true for ongoing growth relationships, like a family or close friendships.

Sue's relationships lack reciprocity, and she hesitates in taking the necessary steps to bring balance to them. "But I don't want to have to *ask* Jim or my friend Betsy to meet my needs. If they care about me, why can't they figure it out without my having to say anything? It would be selfish of me to say anything. Besides, I bend over backward trying to meet their needs. Can't they just for once do something for me?"

When Sue was growing up, she was taught never to express her needs and never to ask for things. Only selfish people did that. But Sue has taken those beliefs into her adult world, where they have crippled her relationships.

Sue needs to change in a variety of ways. She needs to be able to recognize her needs and express them to her close friends and family. She needs to clarify her expectations and give others opportunity and freedom to respond to these expectations without putting guilt on them. She needs the freedom not to give or be responsible if she feels used. (Chapter 8 "Negotiating Contracts" will give further help in moving toward reciprocity in relationships.)

CODEPENDENCY CONFUSION

Probably the most confusing aspect of reciprocity for codependent Christians is that Scripture seems to emphasize giving and to disparage any forms of self-interest. This may lead you to ask whether expecting reciprocity can be right.

God wants his people to have relationships that are healthy, peaceful, and loving. He doesn't desire to put excessive burdens on one member while the other has it easy. Do we have a right to expect reciprocity? Yes! Are we to focus only on giving? No! "Our desire is not that others might be relieved while you are hard pressed, but that there might be equality. At the present time your plenty will supply what they need, so that in turn their plenty will supply what you need. Then there will be equality" (2 Cor. 8:13–14). Justice and equity are a part of God's purposes and values, and he desires to see them in relationships. When one person gives and another takes without reciprocating, that is injustice.

Learning reciprocity also involves learning healthy giving. Sometimes people give with a hidden agenda or unspoken expectation to get love and acceptance in return. And when the gesture is not appreciated or paid back, the giver gets angry or hurt, resulting in feelings of indebtedness and righteous indignation.

The problem is that the giving is an "agreement" of sorts—I'll give you such and such if you do such and such in return. But the agreement is a unilateral one, made only by the codependent. For example, Helen worked hard to fix her husband, Frank, a snack every day after work, and she became upset when he showed no appreciation for her gesture. Frank didn't really want the daily snack and had no idea Helen expected him to pay her back somehow.

LOOK IN THE MIRROR
Put a check next to the characteristics you see in yourself:
- [ ] I am overly responsible
- [ ] I am overly involved
- [ ] I am overly sensitive
- [ ] I need to be needed
- [ ] I am loving
- [ ] I am kind
- [ ] I am patient
- [ ] I am generous
- [ ] I am arrogant
- [ ] I am self-righteous
- [ ] I feel guilty
- [ ] I feel ripped off
- [ ] I feel resentful
- [ ] I feel angry
- [ ] I feel powerless
- [ ] I feel depressed
- [ ] I feel afraid of rejection
- [ ] I feel worthless

RECOVERY STORIES
#1 ENOUGH IS ENOUGH

Carolyn came in for counseling because she felt burned out. "After my mother died, I couldn't give the way I always had in the past. I thought my friends and family would pick up the slack, but nobody did except my husband. If I didn't initiate in my relationships, there was no contact. One friend, I realized, almost never drove or paid when we went out for lunch. I asked her to drive, and she said she thought I was getting selfish since my mother died. That hurt me, and I felt guilty so I went home and cried."

Carolyn had always been a giving person and was well liked in her community. She enjoyed contributing but realized after her mother died that although most everyone could count on her, she could count on hardly anyone. She found herself becoming easily hurt when others overlooked her needs. She knew she needed help, but the only way she tried to get it was to make the other person feel guilty enough to do something for her. Her relationships with her husband, Bob, and her two older children became strained.

The counselor helped Carolyn face her grief in losing her mother and helped her begin to make the adjustments needed in her relationships. In facing her new limitations, Carolyn needed to be more direct with her expectations. That was hard for Carolyn to do. She said, "God wants me to give without expecting anything in return." The counselor helped her to see that there was a time for that type of giving but also a time for reciprocity.

Carolyn tried to follow the counselor's advice. She began to ask her friends and family members to help with certain jobs, and she started to voice her needs to Bob. When Carolyn saw her relationships change, she was less depressed. She could also see others growing now that she did less giving. The changes were slow but significant for Carolyn. Bob said, "Carolyn was always so willing and capable. I just mainly got out of her way. Now I feel I contribute more. I didn't like this at first, but now I feel God has helped us both."

1. **What were Carolyn's beliefs *before* recovery?**
   a. I have to be responsible for everything.
   b. My needs don't count.
   c. People like me only if I do all the giving.

2. **What were her changed beliefs *in* recovery?**
   a. I'm not the only one responsible for my relationships. I can count on God and others to contribute too.
   b. My needs also count, and sometimes God wants me to be a receiver.
   c. I can be liked even when I have needs and don't do all the giving.

3. **What were Carolyn's dominant feelings *before* recovery?**
   a. Used—the martyr complex
   b. Depression, oversensitivity
   c. Resentment

4. **What were her changed feelings *in* recovery?**
   a. Confidence and assertiveness
   b. Openness to receive
   c. Security

5. **What were Carolyn's behavior patterns *before* recovery?**

a. Laying guilt trips on others—"I'm the only one in this relationship who ever initiates."
   b. Denying her own needs
   c. Expecting other people to know her needs

6. What were her changed behavior patterns *in* recovery?
   a. Taking responsibility to look at angry feelings and make requests about desires
   b. Clarifying expectations and developing clearer agreements in relationships
   c. Developing more reciprocity in relationships through allowing others to give back to her

#2 LARGE MARGE

Once upon a time there was a rather large woman named Marge. Everybody liked Marge, and Marge liked everybody. Marge was married to an ugly little ogre named Demando, who was very selfish. Marge's mother was similar to Demando in that she also acted like an ogre, especially when she drank too much juice from fermented berries. To get along with her mother, Marge had learned as a child to give and be good in order not to be yelled at.

Marge and Demando had a daughter named Demanda. This little family lived out in the woods in the enchanted forest. Marge worked very hard for her family, carrying water from the well, baking, cooking, baking, cooking, and then baking some more. In fact, baking was Marge's favorite activity, especially because she liked to eat the cookies and pies—all of them.

Marge loved her daughter, Demanda, very much and felt sorry for her because her father was always so mean to her. To help Demanda, large Marge decided to support her and not to make any demands on her. When Marge was frustrated with her husband's behavior, she just ate more cookies and more pies.

A few years later there was a rash of divorces in the enchanted forest, especially among ogres, and Marge and Demando parted company. Marge gained custody of Demanda, who was a young woman by then, sweet but exasperatingly stubborn.

Marge soon became depressed because Demanda did nothing to help her around the house. She sat around all day while Marge did all the work. Rather than say anything to Demanda, Marge just ate more cookies.

One day Marge asked Demanda to help her with the laundry.

CODEPENDENCY CONFUSION

Demanda refused to help and accused Marge of not loving her. Crushed, Marge began to cry. Demanda stomped out of the cottage in disgust. In despair, Marge cried out, "You're as stubborn as a mule!"

With a flash of brilliant light, Demanda changed into a mule. A fairy godmother appeared and said to Marge, "For one year Demanda will work for you and carry all your burdens, but you have to command this in her. Tell her what you need, and expect her to do it. If she becomes obedient, she will return to human form, become a princess, and honor her mother. If she stays stubborn, she will remain a mule." (The fairy godmother worked part-time in a counseling agency.)

Marge worked hard to become more assertive and direct in telling Demanda what she expected of her. Demanda soon responded to her mother's requests and agreed to do some of the work. After a year, a soft-hearted Demanda reappeared, and they lived happily ever after, with occasional visits from the fairy godmother to keep their recovery in line.

1. What were Marge's beliefs *before* recovery?

2. What were her changed beliefs *in* recovery?

3. What were Marge's dominant feelings *before* recovery?

4. What were her changed feelings *in* recovery?

5. What were Marge's behavior patterns *before* recovery?

6. What were her changed behavior patterns *in* recovery?

7. How are you like Marge?

RECOVERY PROBERS

1. How can you check to see if your expectations are too high or too low?

2. Which of your expectations are unmet? What expectations of others are you not meeting? Can you negotiate these?

3. Do you need to be more assertive with your expectations? Do you need to surrender them to God? How can you know which to do?

4. How do you keep yourself in a role where you do all or most of the giving in your relationships?

5. What is the most difficult part for you of dealing with reciprocity?

6. Which of your relationships are healthy, with givers and receivers? Which are unhealthy?

RECOVERY GUIDE

The Scriptures communicate that you should give because you want to, not because of compulsion. Giving comes from your values and convictions.

Read 2 Corinthians 9:7–8.

1. What does it mean to give compulsively?

2. How is giving cheerfully different from giving reluctantly or under compulsion?

3. How does the instruction that "each man should give what he has decided in his heart to give" allow the believer freedom from external pressures and internal "shoulds"?

4. How does this advice about giving translate into your relationships?

5. In what relationships are you giving under compulsion?

RECOVERY GOALS

1. In which relationships do you need to ask for reciprocity?

2. How can you do this?

3. What needs do you need to articulate? To whom?

4. What would keep you from following through with asking for reciprocity?

5. How can you stop making people indebted to you?

4. The Overreactor: Give Up Anxiety

RECOVERY FOCUS

- Minimize anxiety instead of amplifying it, trusting God with your fears.
- Recognize and manage stress in your life.
- Learn to discern major stress from minor stress.

RECOVERY INFORMATION

A fourth role codependents play is that of the overreactor, who sees all of life as a major calamity. Do you overreact? Do you get adrenaline highs from talking about conflict—yours or other people's conflict? If you play this role, your life probably feels as if it's always chaotic and out of control. You may find you spend most of your energy reacting to circumstances and coping with stress.

Overreactors often come from abusive families. Having lived with threats, they now see them everywhere. What is an irritation for others becomes a catastrophe for them. Because they are overly serious, overreactors should work on developing a sense of humor and learn to relax and trust God with their lives.

This chapter will help you move out of the state of reaction. You will learn how to disengage from it and to feel safe, relaxed, and secure. Growth in this area means learning how to apply Psalm 18:2 to your relationships: "The Lord is my rock, my fortress and my deliverer; my God is my rock, in whom I take refuge. He is my shield and the horn of my salvation, my stronghold."

Dr. Murray Bowen describes the overreactor as an amplifier of family anxiety. The amplifier maximizes crises and thrives on talking about "how bad it is."

LOOK IN THE MIRROR

Read the following characteristics and check those that describe you:

- [ ] I am very sensitive to stress and tension.
- [ ] I get irritated or afraid quickly.
- [ ] I exaggerate.
- [ ] I need someone to talk to in order to feel safe.
- [ ] I get energy by talking about crisis.
- [ ] I dwell on bad situations.
- [ ] I seem always to be in crisis.
- [ ] My friends are constantly in crisis.
- [ ] I feel anxious.
- [ ] I feel a sense of impending doom.
- [ ] I feel sad.
- [ ] I feel helpless.
- [ ] I feel victimized.

If you find you are an overreactor, interacting with a support group will help you see reality more clearly, giving you a barometer of your personal level of reactivity and anxiety. The group members can help you discern which of your stresses are major and which are minor.

CODEPENDENCY CONFUSION

The confusion in this issue comes from deciding how to handle your overreaction. The Bible says, "Don't worry about anything." Do you just repress your anxieties and try to make them go away? Or should you talk about them, even though that may increase your anxiety?

Overreaction and intense anxiety often happen because you are anxious over something you aren't in touch with. You may deny your feelings only to find you are driven by them. Other Christians tend to encourage this denial by telling you not to worry.

The psalmist encourages us to examine our thoughts and feelings so that they can be resolved and healed. "Search me, O God, and know my heart; test me and know my anxious thoughts. See if there is any offensive way in me, and lead me in the way everlasting" (Ps. 139:23–24). Working through feelings to a resolve is a process that takes time and energy, but it brings rest to the soul.

When you learn to curb your reactive style, you will make your relationships safer for others. If you can feel secure instead of rejected, hurt, or angry, the atmosphere becomes safe for both.

RECOVERY STORIES
#1 CHICKEN LITTLE

Jane was an adult child of alcoholic parents. Her father was volatile and abused her both verbally and physically. Jane seemed afraid of everything. She didn't have much self-confidence and was always questioning authority. Jane was sure if she didn't do everything "right," her children would turn out to be failures.

Jane came to counseling because Jay, her youngest child, had failed algebra. Jay was angry at his mom because she had made a big deal of his failing grade and had told all her friends about her son's "catastrophe." Jay felt it was none of their business. This was the first course Jay had ever failed; most of his grades were average.

When Jane talked with the counselor, she was distraught. Wringing her hands, she said, "I know if Jay doesn't straighten up, he won't make it through high school." She pressured Jay to stop seeing some of his friends and to take down some of the posters he had on his bedroom walls. Jane read many articles about problem teenagers, always sure that Jay would turn out just like the hopeless teenager in the article. Jane's husband, Tony, constantly told her not to worry, which only made Jane feel as if he didn't care.

The counselor told Jane to practice not worrying. She thought this was "bad advice" but practiced it anyway, praying that God would help her sort out her worries and help her give up those that were out of balance and unhealthy. Through counseling Jane began to realize that she was afraid and irritated about most of what Jay did and said. She didn't like his hair, his attitude, or his friends. She was sure each of his decisions brought him closer to ruin. The counselor helped her develop a sense of humor and see Jay's decisions as less threatening. She made a list of all the irritants she had with Jay and began to ask herself, "What difference will this make a hundred years from now?" She also asked her husband to help Jay with his algebra homework, and Tony took over. Jane began to feel as if she could relax more around Jay.

1. **What were Jane's beliefs *before* recovery?**
    a. Whatever can go wrong will go wrong.
    b. Something slightly wrong will always lead to some major catastrophe.

c. Telling people about my worries is the only way to diminish my anxiety.

2. What were her new beliefs *in* recovery?
   a. God can change bad appearances into good results.
   b. Just because something or someone is off base doesn't mean it or they will end in tragedy.
   c. I can reduce my anxieties by trusting God, talking them over with a godly friend, and not focusing on them all the time, which sometimes increases their power in my life.

3. What were Jane's dominant feelings *before* recovery?
   a. Sense of constant dread or threat
   b. Anxiety and worry
   c. Irritability and overreaction

4. What were her changed feelings *in* recovery?
   a. Sense of hope
   b. Relief and relaxation
   c. Warmth and affection

5. What were Jane's behavior patterns *before* recovery?
   a. Nagging about other people's behavior
   b. Obsessively looking for and discussing wrongs and potential wrongs
   c. Venting anxiety and anger on others with negative beliefs and criticisms

6. What were her changed behavior patterns *in* recovery?
   a. Confronting the major issues with power (like having Tony work with Jay on his algebra)
   b. Disengaging from minor irritants (like hair, clothes, attitude, etc.) and relaxing around Jay
   c. Limiting who she talks to about Jay's problems, respecting Jay's privacy and need for confidentiality

#2 AN EYE FOR AN EYE

Martha and Richard were in constant battle with each other. Both had problems with drugs and alcohol. Martha had been sober for a year and a half, but Richard thought he "didn't have a problem." Once or twice a month he would go out drinking with the guys from work.

When Richard would go out, Martha would get anxious about his drinking, and her feelings would escalate until she was in a rage. When Richard came home, Martha would attack him with a vengeance, yelling and screaming. Richard would retaliate by screaming back at her. Eventually Martha would walk out of the room crying, going to her oldest daughter for comfort and support.

Martha told her support group, "I can't control my feelings; I get so angry." The group members shared from their own experiences.

One woman said "I found what I couldn't control was my husband's drinking, but I could disengage my reactions to it."

"How do you do that?" Martha asked.

The woman replied, "Well, I felt justified in yelling at my husband because I hated his drinking, kind of an eye-for-an-eye, yelling for drinking. But I decided that my behavior was neither justified nor helpful. Since I hate the smell of alcohol on his breath, I decided that if he drinks, I'll just stay away from him. It worked. I haven't been yelling for over a year. I feel better about myself and disengaged from those reactive kind of feelings."

Martha went home from the group and decided she would work on disengaging. She came back to tell the group about her first victory.

"When Richard went out, I started getting anxious. I thought, *We're just going to fight again.* I decided I would distract myself, so I started to write a letter I'd been putting off. It worked. I wrote until nine o'clock and then watched television. I went to bed an hour and a half later, but I soon began to worry again. Then I prayed, read a Scripture passage, and fell asleep. I'm sure Richard was surprised because he asked me the next morning whether everything was okay. I said, 'I'm fine. I don't like your drinking, but you already know that.' He reacted to what I said in the same old way, but I didn't fight back, and we had a pleasant day."

Martha gained the courage to disengage and find some safety from the reactivity of her relationship.

1. **What were Martha's beliefs *before* recovery?**

2. **What were her changed beliefs *in* recovery?**

3. **What were Martha's dominant feelings *before* recovery?**

4. What were her changed feelings *in* recovery?

5. What were Martha's behavior patterns *before* recovery?

6. What were her changed behavior patterns *in* recovery?

7. How are you like Martha?

RECOVERY PROBERS

1. To what minor issues are you reacting?

2. What major issue may you be overlooking?

3. Are you justifying your overreaction? How?

4. Are you amplifying situations in your life above their intensity? How?

5. To whom do you exaggerate your problems and injustices?

6. What stressors in your life may you be overlooking?

RECOVERY GUIDE

When the psalmist experienced anxiety, he talked about God in ways that brought security and protection to his heart and soul. God was his protector, provider, fortress, refuge, rock, and deliverer.

Choose one (or all) of the following psalms and read it aloud, substituting your name for all the personal pronouns. Example: "The Lord is Randy's light and Randy's salvation. Whom shall Randy fear?" Psalm 27, Psalm 34, Psalm 37, Psalm 91.

Read Romans 12:17–21.
1. What are you to do with your angry or vengeful feelings?

2. How can you make letting go a reality in your life? Would it help to write down what you wish to give to God?

Read Matthew 23:23–24.
1. How is Jesus saying these people are overlooking the majors and focusing on minors?

2. What issue are you willing to give to God today?

Read Romans 14:17–19.
1. In this passage, what are the majors, and what are the minors?

2. What minors do you let come between you and others?

RECOVERY GOALS
1. In which relationship are you caught in a reactive cycle?

2. When will you be willing to break out of that cycle?

3. How will you do that?

4. What do you feel today, and how will you work those feelings through with God?

5. When you know what is right or godly, how do you let God walk with you to a place where your heart feels that too?

6. What are some ways you can disengage emotionally?

7. What do you need spiritually to calm your heart? How will you find rest and safety in God? When?

8. How can you reduce stress in your life?

5. The Controller: Give Up Dominance

RECOVERY FOCUS

- Give up trying to change others.
- Move from controlling others to respecting them.
- Respect yourself by trusting other people.

RECOVERY INFORMATION

The fifth role codependents can play is that of the controller, the person who tends to dominate others in order to feel secure and valuable. Hank struggles with his controlling role. He is frustrated by his daughter's behavior and feels that by applying enough pressure, he can change her. He keeps a close watch on all her activities and relationships and tries to control who she sees and where she goes. When she resists his control, he issues ultimatums. Hank ends up feeling frustrated, angry, and irritated, usually resulting in an emotional cutoff with his daughter.

If you feel you struggle with this role, this chapter will help you move

—from trying to control to showing respect for others.
—from acting like a parent to respecting others' boundaries.
—from arguing to get your way to making requests.
—from acting hard and angry to showing your soft side.

LOOK IN THE MIRROR

Read the following characteristics and check those that describe you:

- [ ] I often use words like "should" and "ought."
- [ ] I'm critical, pointing out where the other person falls short.

- [ ] I invade other people's lives by judging their motives and intentions.
- [ ] I'm cold and distant when I want control or feel irritated.
- [ ] I'm argumentative and confrontational.
- [ ] I use force or forceful behavior, like yelling, threats, venting anger, breaking things, or hitting people.

CODEPENDENCY CONFUSION

The myth of this role is "I can control or change another person's personality or behavior by using certain forceful behavior patterns." The truth is, the attempts to control only lead to a power struggle that destroys the relationship. The power struggle sets up a cycle of action and reaction that almost always ends up in a no-win situation, with one person feeling resentment and the other feeling guilt. The confusion lies in the fact that we may feel it is our job to change others, but our attempts to do so only make things worse. Yet we keep on trying to change others because we do not know what else to do. For the Christian, getting off the merry-go-round involves growing in humility, honesty, and trust of God and the other person.

RECOVERY STORIES

#1 OUT OF CONTROL

Bill, a single parent who had raised several children almost by himself, was having trouble with his nineteen-year-old son, Larry. Larry had been in trouble with the law for several years and couldn't seem to hold a job. Bill was bothered when he came home from work and found Larry just lying around the house, doing nothing.

Bill was frustrated in his attempts to get Larry to act responsibly. He tried sarcasm. He tried intimidation. He tried yelling, threatening, and issuing ultimatums. But Larry didn't change. He only retaliated with verbal attacks.

Bill loved Larry and was afraid of losing him. Hurt by Larry's verbal abuse, Bill wanted to give up. He said, "I'm just plain tired of fighting. I think I'm too old for parenting."

In actuality, Bill depended on Larry and was afraid of Larry's disapproval, and that fear crippled his ability to be firm with Larry. Through counseling, Bill began to see that he needed to respect himself more and to quit telling Larry what he should do. He quit lecturing and required Larry to get a job no matter what the consequences. Bill eventually said, "If you want to lie in bed all day, that's up to you, but not in my house. I'm not willing to support you if you won't work. I've talked with your mother, and you can move over there."

Larry got mad, persecuted Bill, and moved out to live with his mother, an alcoholic. Bill was sad and worried about Larry. Bill would slip into controlling, suggestive statements like, "If you live with her, you're going to be just like her." Then he would catch himself and apologize.

After a year, Larry asked to move back, but Bill refused unless Larry got a job. Larry became angry, but got a job and moved into an apartment with two other guys. Bill had to risk the loss of the relationship in order to allow emotional independence to develop. He was afraid of losing Larry but began to trust God and was willing to let go. Bill and Larry gradually began to spend more time together, doing things like fishing and going to ball games.

1. **What were Bill's beliefs *before* recovery?**
   a. I can change Larry by yelling, attacking, threatening, and issuing ultimatums.
   b. If I complain enough, Larry will change.
   c. Expressing anger through sarcasm is better than being direct and causing a confrontation.

2. **What were his changed beliefs *in* recovery?**
   a. I need to decide what I'm willing to put up with and quit complaining, thereby regaining some self-respect through boundaries and limits.
   b. Using sarcasm, yelling, threats, and predicting Larry's future negatively makes things worse rather than better.
   c. It's hard for me to be direct, but I have to be willing to pay a price if I'm going to get Larry to pay a price.

3. **What were Bill's dominant feelings *before* recovery?**
   a. Resentment, hurt, feeling used
   b. Anger that Larry wouldn't change
   c. Depression over Larry's stubbornness and unwillingness to get out of bed; feelings of being a failure

4. **What are his changed feelings *in* recovery?**
   a. Loss from letting go and trusting God; sadness, anger, grief
   b. Relief from tension

c. More self-esteem and dignity from setting a boundary

5. What were Bill's behavior patterns *before* recovery?
   a. Yelling, threatening, sarcasm, and using intimidation
   b. Trading off personal dignity and boundaries for friendship
   c. Unwillingness to fight and to assert authority as a parent

6. What were his changed behavior patterns *in* recovery?
   a. Deciding to pick a boundary and follow through on it
   b. Respecting his own limitations and feelings of frustration by communicating unwillingness to have Larry lie around without a job
   c. Maintaining a boundary even when it cost Bill his main alliance

#2 VILLAGE OF AMF

Queen Blamer lived in a small castle in a village called Amf, which meant it "Ain't my fault." Queen Blamer was a beautiful woman, but true to her name, she was somewhat unblameable. The only predictable quality about her was that you could be assured if something went wrong, it wasn't her fault. And if you were around, you would be blamed.

The queen's behavior affected the whole village. If you went to the baker to get a cake you ordered and it wasn't ready, he would say, "If you had been more clear about when you wanted it, I would have had it ready." It almost seemed as if everyone in Amf had eyes that could see what others did wrong but were blind to their own wrongs.

Queen Blamer was also gifted in having a quick mind. She could tell her court why something wasn't her fault and put the blame on someone else almost before most people could add up three numbers. She felt strongly that her reactions were justified and helpful in keeping "order" in Amf.

One day a humble old woman named Iowna walked into Amf. She didn't look like much. Her clothes were torn, her hair was gray, and her face was worn and wrinkly. She had a sparkle in her eye, though, and a clarity that was beyond anything in Amf.

Iowna went to the city magistrate to pay the city tax of ten guffs a week in order to be able to stay in Amf. She gave the magistrate a twenty-guff bill, and he gave her back fifteen guffs without realizing he was giving her too much. When the magistrate added up his guffs at the end of the day, he realized Iowna had taken five guffs too much. He quickly had her arrested and brought before the queen.

THE CONTROLLER: GIVE UP DOMINANCE 47

Queen Blamer confronted Iowna and said, "You are accused of stealing five guffs from Amf. How do you plead?" Of course, everyone expected Iowna to blame the magistrate, because that's how people behaved in Amf.

Iowna thought carefully and replied slowly, "I did take five more guffs in change than was due me, and I'm sorry. I'm willing to pay my dues. I didn't recount my money until after I was arrested."

Queen Blamer had expected Iowna to resist the arrest and accusation and almost fell off her throne when Iowna acknowledged her blame. Unprepared for Iowna's response, Queen Blamer yelled anyway, "This is all your fault!"

Iowna looked Queen Blamer in the eye, which no one ever did in Amf, with a look that seemed to penetrate all the way into the queen's heart. Iowna's reply was gentle but direct. "No, I think the magistrate also overlooked the counting of the change."

The queen was so struck by the look Iowna had given her that she crumbled on the spot. It seemed that an archaic structure of rules and thinking also crumbled that day. The magistrate and Iowna split the five guffs; for the first time, the queen's judgment was just and true. Queen Blamer apologized for yelling and then hired Iowna as an advisor. In the end, Queen Blamer's rule became as beautiful as her appearance.

1. **What were Queen Blamer's beliefs *before* recovery?**

2. **What were her changed beliefs *in* recovery?**

3. **What were Queen Blamer's dominant feelings *before* recovery?**

4. **What were her changed feelings *in* recovery?**

5. **What were Queen Blamer's behavior patterns *before* recovery?**

6. What were her changed behavior patterns *in* recovery?

7. How are you like Queen Blamer?

RECOVERY PROBERS

1. What relationships are you trying to control?

2. What are your controlling behavior patterns (fear, guilt, helplessness, etc.)?

3. What do you feel about yourself when you act in a controlling way?

4. How do you blame and fail to take ownership for your part? Do you listen to others to hear how you affect them? Do they hear you?

5. If you're in a parent role with a child, how can you establish a boundary and set up a consequence if the boundary is broken? What keeps you from following through with this?

6. How can you empower others to change? Example: Allow them to own the responsibility without nagging; just believe they are capable.

7. How can you be more relaxed, flexible, and fun in relationships?

RECOVERY GUIDE

The religious controllers of Christ's day were the Pharisees and Sadducees. Christ sharply addresses them about their pride, judgmental and critical attitudes, and rigidity.

Read Matthew 7:1−5.
1. What is Christ's main point?

2. Whom are you told to be responsible to change?

Read Luke 6:36−45.
1. How does focusing on another person's faults blind you to your own?

2. Toward whom do you feel the most critical? How can you make amends for that?

Read Luke 6:1−11.
1. How were the Pharisees being rigid?

2. How are you rigid and inflexible?

RECOVERY GOALS
1. Whom do you need to give up trying to control?

2. What kind of limits do you need for self-respect? Do you need to establish some space between you and the person you tend to control? How will you do that?

3. When will you take the first step to give up control? (If your answer is now, pray and ask God for help.)

4. What would prevent you from letting go of your controlling behavior patterns? What will you do about it?

6. Dealing with Guilt

RECOVERY FOCUS

- Discern the difference between true guilt and false guilt.
- Give up feeling guilty for other people's problems.
- Learn to disengage instead of internalizing other people's feelings.

RECOVERY INFORMATION

Now that you've examined the various roles codependents play, you will learn to practice some essential coping strategies: dealing with guilt, setting boundaries, negotiating contracts, breaking negative patterns through intervention, and finding love in healthy ways.

This chapter will explore the dynamics of dealing with guilt. When someone criticizes you, do you take it personally and feel attacked? When someone near you is angry—even if the anger isn't directed at you—do you feel guilty? When something goes wrong, do you hang your head, apologize profusely, and feel like putting on sackcloth and ashes?

If this describes you, you need to practice two important coping skills: disengaging when you feel attacked and resisting the instinct to internalize someone else's anger. When you disengage, you view the other person's anger as that person's problem, not yours. You no longer get hooked emotionally into feeling guilty or defensive about other people's anger.

CODEPENDENCY CONFUSION

The confusion in this codependency issue arises from our understanding of *guilt*. True guilt comes as a result of sin, breaking God's law and violating his will for our lives. In that sense, we *are* guilty. And God takes that guilt seriously enough to pay for it with the death of his guiltless Son.

But is the guilt that Christ bore the same guilt codependents feel? No. Much of the guilt codependents feel is false guilt, or blame.

You may live in an environment that is saturated with blame. The blame you feel often has little to do with anything but someone's venting anger. You may have accepted a scapegoat role and feel overly responsible, willing to accept the guilt of your entire family. You may feel that if only you would try hard enough, you could make everybody happy, cause the rain to stop, and pay off the national debt.

When you realize you don't have to accept or internalize the other person's blame, anger, or disapproval, you will begin to experience freedom. God's desire is not to oppress you with guilt so that you despair and feel miserable. Jesus said, "I have come that [you] may have life, and have it to the full" (John 10:10).

RECOVERY STORIES

#1 PEACEMAKER

Matt had grown up playing the peacemaker in his family. When he married Rebecca, who had come from a physically and emotionally abusive family, he had some adjustments to make. When Rebecca was stressed, she often blew up, yelling and expressing anger openly—regardless of who it affected.

Matt's response was to feel as if her reactions were his fault. Any accusation with an element of truth in it left him off balance, introspective, and withdrawn.

In a codependency group, Matt found others who felt the same feelings: worthlessness, powerlessness, guilt, and fear. He saw other codependents realize that their weakness and guilt helped to encourage the dominance of others. Matt decided that his behavior only made it easier for Rebecca to vent her anger without regard for his response, so he decided he needed to stand up to her. He began to express his own feelings, and when Rebecca was angry, instead of placating her or looking for a place to hide, he became more detached from her anger.

One day, when Rebecca was cleaning the garage, she got frustrated and began to blow up. The old Matt would have picked up the frustration and tried to calm her, make her feel different, or leave. The new Matt stayed and watched as she got angrier. Rebecca then turned and said, "Matt, you never do anything around here!"

Matt realized he was not to blame for her feelings, so he disengaged and said, "You think it's all my fault you're angry."

Rebecca said, "Yes!" as she kicked a paint can.

Matt replied in a matter-of-fact tone, "It seems to me, Rebec when you get angry, you blame me. And I don't like it."

"If you would do something around here, I wouldn't be so frustrated!" Rebecca snapped.

"I don't do anything?" retorted Matt.

"No. You never do anything!" Rebecca said with hostility.

Matt said, "Is this about you being frustrated with how the garage looks or are you trying to tell me something?"

"I want some help," said Rebecca.

"Then ask me. I'd rather be asked than blamed," said Matt.

"You never do anything I ask," retorted Rebecca.

"Try me," replied Matt.

"If you can't see I need help, then forget it. It's not worth it," she said accusingly.

"Rebecca, I'm not going to feel guilty over your frustration. If you want something, then ask. Otherwise, I'm going into the house."

"Well, go then. You don't care anyway!" yelled Rebecca.

So Matt left.

1. **What were Matt's beliefs *before* recovery?**
   a. I have to keep the peace, and I'm responsible to keep Rebecca from frustration.
   b. All anger is bad, and I can't live with it.
   c. I have to feel guilty when Rebecca is angry with me and placate her.

2. **What were his changed beliefs *in* recovery?**
   a. I'm responsible for dealing with my feelings, and Rebecca is responsible for hers.
   b. It's okay to be angry, and I won't die if Rebecca expresses her anger or frustration.
   c. I don't have to feel guilty when Rebecca is angry.

3. **What were Matt's dominant feelings *before* recovery?**
   a. Guilt
   b. Fear
   c. Tension and defensiveness

4. **What were his changed feelings *in* recovery?**
   a. Sense of relief or freedom
   b. Honesty
   c. Security and caring

5. What were Matt's behavior patterns *before* recovery?
   a. Internalizing anger and placating Rebecca to ease tension
   b. Stuffing anger and withdrawing
   c. Becoming introspective ("If only I could be good enough.") and feeling depressed

6. What were his changed behavior patterns *in* recovery?
   a. Asserting himself in dialogue
   b. Staying disengaged while remaining open and honest
   c. Giving Rebecca choices and working toward mutual respect

#2 BORN TO BE BLAMED

Grace was the only child of an angry, abusive mother. From early on Grace's mother would say things like, "You ruined my life. If only I hadn't had you, I'd be happy." Grace internalized those statements and felt guilty about existing. The only thing that seemed to make her feel better was to help others. The problem was that Grace attracted people with problems, people who often manipulated her through guilt.

One of these people was Sally, a woman who had an addiction to prescription medication. She would call Grace and want to talk for hours. When Grace would try to get off the phone, Sally would accuse her of not caring. To avoid feeling guilty, Grace would talk to Sally well into the night, resulting in her inability to function at work.

While Grace was in counseling, she realized that if someone got angry with her or put blame on her, she would automatically yield in order to please. Grace began to learn how to disengage by first listening and then simply being honest. One night on the phone with Sally, she said, "Sally, it's late, and I need to go to bed."

Sally retorted, "Some Christians wouldn't care if I were dying."

Grace replied, "Sally, I care, but I'm tired. I'm going to bed. Good-night."

Grace said, "In the past I would have had to call up and ask forgiveness to appease Sally's anger, but last night I felt okay." Grace began to find other ways to feel worthwhile besides helping others, and she took classes at a community college to help her career and personal interests.

1. What were Grace's beliefs *before* recovery?

2. What were her changed beliefs *in* recovery?

DEALING WITH GUILT

3. What were Grace's dominant feelings *before* recovery?

4. What were her changed feelings *in* recovery?

5. What were Grace's behavior patterns *before* recovery?

6. What were her changed behavior patterns *in* recovery?

7. How are you like Grace?

RECOVERY PROBERS

1. What is true guilt?

2. What is false guilt?

3. How do you know when you are being codependent in your guilt feelings?

4. How can you disengage when someone is blaming you?

5. If you feel responsible for everything or everyone's feelings, what can you do?

6. What if you really are responsible and someone is blaming you? What can you do?

7. How do you blame others?

RECOVERY GUIDE
Read 2 Corinthians 7:10.

Some theologians say that the Scripture never intends to produce guilt and that this passage referring to sorrow clarifies the concept. It refers to a godly sorrow that "leads to salvation," "leaves no regret," and contrasts with a worldly sorrow that "brings death." The purpose of sorrow here is to bring a godly change, while worldly sorrow seems to bring no change, only bad feelings.

1. What is Paul's intention in making the Corinthians sorrowful?

2. Do you believe God wants to weigh you down with guilt?

Read 1 Corinthians 4:2–5.

1. Paul has been judged by some of the Corinthians, but he refuses to internalize their criticism and feel bad or introspective about it. Does Paul say he is not guilty?

2. How does Paul gain freedom from the Corinthians' criticism?

Read Galatians 5:1.

Paul communicates clearly in Galatians that Christians are to be free from the oppression of the Law. This oppression was a clear injunction to value freedom and not to be manipulated through fear or guilt.

1. What does he mean when he says, "Do not let yourselves be burdened again by a yoke of slavery"?

2. How could this principle apply to your burdening yourself by guilt that is oppressive? How could you stand firm?

RECOVERY GOALS

1. How does God see you? Make a list of positive affirmations based on Psalm 139 and Isaiah 43:1–7.

2. Who blames you? Exaggerate that person's blame to yourself until it seems ridiculous to you. Example: If someone says to you, "You never help around here," write down an exaggerated response, "You're right. I never do anything. In fact, it's amazing I even put the energy into breathing." Exaggerate until you find it funny and it loses its sting.

3. What can you do to disengage from guilt?

4. When will you start?

5. What would prevent you from freeing yourself from guilt? What will you do about it?

7. Setting Boundaries

RECOVERY FOCUS

- Respect yourself enough to protect yourself.
- Discern what boundaries you need to set in order to stay emotionally healthy.
- Learn to say no without losing the relationship.

RECOVERY INFORMATION

Do you have a hard time saying no to people? When the phone sales representative calls, do you feel obligated to buy something? When someone asks you for a favor, do you say yes and then resent them? Do you yield and do things you really do not believe in or want to do?

Many codependents are only able to establish boundaries when they become fed up with a bad relationship. Then they set boundaries out of resentment, not because they care about the relationship. In fact, their "boundary" actually becomes an emotional or physical cut-off.

Boundaries protect relationships because they protect the dignity of the individuals involved. Boundaries also allow us to say no, which gives us freedom. When we are free to choose, then we can say yes from our hearts.

LOOK IN THE MIRROR

Read the following characteristics and check those that describe you:

- [ ] I find it difficult to express my own desires.
- [ ] I rarely let other people know what I think.
- [ ] I have low self-esteem.
- [ ] I get angry when other people intrude on my life.
- [ ] I often withdraw without talking.

- [ ] I often feel violated and used.
- [ ] I feel fearful.
- [ ] I feel resentful of other people's demands.

CODEPENDENCY CONFUSION

The confusion is that Christians often feel that saying no, setting boundaries, or protecting themselves is wrong, mean, and selfish. After all, doesn't Scripture counsel us to be self-sacrificing? How can you be a Christian *and* be self-protective?

Your inability to say no may stem from a variety of sources. If as a child you suffered abuse, which violated your personal boundaries, you may not respect your own boundaries as an adult. You may have been punished for setting boundaries and now feel it isn't worth the struggle. Your low self-esteem may make you afraid of other people's disapproval and prevent you from saying no and risking disapproval without support. Or you may feel afraid of retaliation and cower rather than express any self-respect.

This chapter will help you gain inner strength, self-respect, and courage to set healthy, reasonable boundaries. Again, remember that the key idea is *balance*. Setting boundaries doesn't mean you're going to become a self-centered, demanding person.

By learning to set boundaries, you will reduce your need to become angry and resentful when other people intrude on your life. Establishing these boundaries means you have to communicate directly and clearly about what you feel and are and are not willing to do.

If you begin to change your role by setting boundaries, you also need to continue to invest in the relationship in other areas. For example: "I'm not willing to hear you complain about her any more. (Boundary) Let's talk about something else. How was your day at work?" (Investment)

RECOVERY STORIES

#1 PLEASE-DON'T-HURT-ME VS. STOMP-ON-YOU

Once upon a time there was a woman named Please-Don't-Hurt-Me, who lived in a small town named Fragile. Please-Don't-Hurt-Me had a small house and a tiny garden, which was surrounded by a barely visible fence.

Fragile also was home to a man named Stomp-on-You. About twice a week Stomp-on-You would march through the town and destroy some of Please-Don't-Hurt-Me's things. The townspeople all felt afraid of Stomp-on-You, and they believed the only way to deal with him was to get out of his way or be nice. They were sure that any resistance would only escalate his anger.

After years of being stomped on, Please-Don't-Hurt-Me was fed up. "I'm moving out of Fragile," she said with determination. Her friends pleaded with her not to go, but Please-Don't-Hurt-Me said, "The only way I'll stay is if my life can be protected. I want to build a fence that Stomp-on-You can't trample."

The neighbors were afraid, and so was Please-Don't-Hurt-Me, but they built a fence. A few days later, Stomp-on-You saw the fence, knocked it down, and trampled the garden. Please-Don't-Hurt-Me felt powerless and discouraged. She vowed once again to leave Fragile.

Then a neighbor named Courage came to her and said, "You have to build a stronger fence. This time build a wall high enough that Stomp-on-You can't knock it down." Please-Don't-Hurt-Me took Courage's advice and gathered her friends to help her build a wall. She assured them, "This wall should never keep you out of my house. That's why I am building a gate. Remember, the wall is for Stomp-on-You."

The townspeople worked hard, and this time when Stomp-on-You approached, he was stopped by the wall. Stomp-on-You didn't like being walled out of Please-Don't-Hurt-Me's life, and he finally realized that she was serious about not letting him trample her garden and property. Please-Don't-Hurt-Me told him that she would keep up the wall but that when she could trust him to come on her property without trampling the garden and destroying her possessions, she would consider allowing him in the gate.

After several months, Please-Don't-Hurt-Me changed her name to Dignity. Stomp-on-You still came around twice a week, and he soon learned to respect Dignity. She occasionally let him in the gate, and they became friends, but not without a lot of work. The townspeople saw the changes in Stomp-on-You's life, and they renamed him Respectful.

1. **What were Please-Don't-Hurt-Me's beliefs *before* recovery?**
    a. It's wrong or selfish to protect myself.
    b. My job is to keep Stomp-on-You from getting angry.
    c. I'm helpless.

2. **What were her changed beliefs *in* recovery?**
    a. If I don't protect myself and make my boundaries clear, others will walk on me.

b. It is Stomp-on-You's job to be respectful and have self-control.
   c. I can set boundaries and protect myself.

3. **What were Please-Don't-Hurt-Me's dominant feelings *before* recovery?**
   a. Fear
   b. Resentment
   c. Guilt

4. **What were her changed feelings *in* recovery?**
   a. Determination
   b. Assertiveness
   c. Power and courage

5. **What were Please-Don't-Hurt-Me's behavior patterns *before* recovery?**
   a. Withdrawing in fear
   b. Avoiding conflict by moving out of Fragile
   c. Depending on the beliefs of others

6. **What were her changed behavior patterns *in* recovery?**
   a. Deciding not to tolerate invasion anymore
   b. Building a wall and gaining support from others
   c. Deciding that protecting herself was worth drastic action

#2 VERBAL ABUSE

Charles had grown up with an alcoholic father. When his dad got drunk, he would berate Charles, calling him "no good," "a bum," "stupid." Charles's mom was very fearful and withdrawn and never protected Charles from his dad's anger. Charles loved his mom and believed she was his only source of love.

Charles grew up and married Susan, a very religious and moral woman. However, she used anger to control Charles. When she was stressed, she would yell and tell Charles he was worthless as a husband. "You're selfish. You don't want to help around here. You don't really care about us; you just want to look good to others."

Charles's response was to "keep the peace" and be good enough to keep Susan happy. He paid a high price when he resisted her tyranny, and he finally burned out trying to be "nice enough."

Charles went to a therapist because he felt he was losing his marriage. The therapist had Charles pick one area in which Charles didn't want his wife to control him. Charles said he didn't want to go to church as much as his wife wanted. He began by explaining to his wife that he loved God but he wanted more time at home. She accused him of backsliding and being selfish, but he held his ground, and over a six-month period she finally let go of her attack.

1. What were Charles's beliefs *before* recovery?

2. What were his changed beliefs *in* recovery?

3. What were Charles's dominant feelings *before* recovery?

4. What were his changed feelings *in* recovery?

5. What were Charles's behavior patterns *before* recovery?

6. What were his changed behavior patterns *in* recovery?

7. How are you like Charles?

RECOVERY PROBERS

1. What do you do when you feel invaded, dominated, or pressured?

2. In what areas is it appropriate to establish some self-protection?

3. What are examples of healthy boundaries and unhealthy boundaries?

4. What is the most difficult thing for you in setting boundaries?

5. Is it okay to have flexible boundaries? In what areas? In what areas do you need to have strong boundaries?

6. Do you invade other people's boundaries?

7. How is not setting boundaries disrespectful to yourself? How does it hurt others?

RECOVERY GUIDE

Read Matthew 7:6−12.

1. How does Jesus encourage self-protection?

2. How does Jesus encourage assertiveness?

Read Exodus 18:13−27.

1. How is Moses encouraged to protect himself from wearing out?

2. How do you overextend your limits? Who makes the most demands on you?

Read 2 Thessalonians 3:6–15.

1. How were the Thessalonian Christians instructed to set boundaries on those who wouldn't work?

2. What can you learn from this passage?

RECOVERY GOALS

1. Who most often invades your life?

2. In what area do you allow this invasion or dominance? Is it good for you or the other person?

3. How will you set a boundary? When?

4. What would be an obstacle to setting this boundary? What might the other person do to make you yield? Commit this to God.

WARNING: Don't endanger yourself. If the situation is dangerous, find help in establishing boundaries.

8. Negotiating Contracts

RECOVERY FOCUS

- Recognize what needs to change in a codependent relationship.
- Decide what you are willing to change.
- Negotiate realistic contracts.

RECOVERY INFORMATION

A third strategy for coping with codependent relationships is learning to negotiate contracts with the other person. "Contract? Doesn't that sound a bit formal?" you may say. A contract is any agreement—spoken or unspoken—between two or more people.

You already operate under many contracts, most of them unspoken. You may have an unspoken agreement with a friend: I'll listen to your problems with your alcoholic husband if you listen to my struggles with a rebellious son. You may have unspoken agreements with your spouse: I'll take care of the household management and the children if you take a full-time job. You may have an unspoken agreement with your child: I buy you clothes and magazines, and I expect you to take care of them.

Some agreements are unhealthy, especially those based on rigid roles where one is the helper and the other helpless.

—I won't take care of myself, so you'll have to.
—If you won't give me sex when I want it, I'll get it somewhere else.
—I'm lazy, so I'll let you do the work for me.
—I'll overlook the fact that you're always late for work because I need your loyalty.
—I'll live with your alcoholism because I don't want to live with the punishment you'll give me if I confront you.

Maybe you're stuck in an unhealthy relationship based on

unhealthy unspoken agreements, and you feel hopeless, empty, frustrated, miserable, vulnerable, and exhausted. That's where negotiating a contract may be a helpful tool for getting unstuck. Let's look in on a conversation in which a husband has decided to change the contract with his wife.

Husband: Mary, I'm not willing to go out drinking with you anymore, and I won't get into the car with you if you've been drinking. I still love you and would like to enjoy things together but not with alcohol.
Wife: That's not fair. You always went drinking with me before. If you loved me, you'd drink with me.
Husband: I don't believe drinking with you is loving you anymore. I don't believe it's good for you, me, or the relationship.

Contracts work best when both parties agree and are notified of any changes in the contract. Respect is a key ingredient in changing contracts. Many codependents lack self-respect and submit themselves to dangerous or degrading situations. As they become aware of this, they often change the relationship contract unilaterally.

CODEPENDENCY CONFUSION

Some contracts have to change even if the other person is unhappy with the change. If you choose to grow or change an unhealthy relationship, you need to realize that you are disrupting the system. This is often an ethical problem for Christians because the disruption may move the already dysfunctional relationship to stop functioning altogether. So you feel stuck. If you change, the other person (spouse, child, parent, employee, or friend) may be angry because he or she may feel you are reneging on the relationship.

This is the confusing part for Christians because you may want to become healthy *and* keep the other happy at the same time. If one person changes, the other may be unwilling to accept the change and may end the relationship. For example, "If you don't go drinking with me, I'll get a divorce." This may cause the Christian to go back to drinking with the alcoholic in order not to feel responsible for a divorce. However, the alcoholic or other dysfunctional person is responsible for his or her choices; the codependent is not forcing a spouse into a divorce.

Because of the way relationships work, these changes are difficult and often make both people in the relationship unhappy. The old relationship will die, and with God's help and blessing, a new, healthy one will develop. If you talk about these changes and negotiate the contract, it will be easier. As you come to realize your part in an unhealthy relationship, you may be tempted to change immediately without realizing how your changes affect the other person.

The following list of guidelines may help you as you re-negotiate your relationship contracts.

Guidelines for Negotiating or Changing a Contract
1. Understand the negotiating style of the other person.
2. Be concise and don't say too much.
3. Respect the other person's freedom to say no.
4. Consider your options.
5. Be clear about your convictions. Say no or that you are not willing to do such and such.
6. Ask yourself, Is this a demand or a request?
7. Don't expect the other person to like the contract change.
8. Remember, you can't always get what you want.
9. Are your expectations for a change in the contract realistic? For example, are you expecting a person who doesn't talk much suddenly to become the life of the party?

RECOVERY STORIES
#1 I QUIT BUT YOU CAN'T

After twelve years of marriage, Ann and Tim have several children. Both parents work outside the home, but Ann does most of the domestic chores. This has frustrated Ann, but she hasn't known what to do about it.

Through an ACOA (Adult Children of Alcoholics) support group Ann attends, she discovered that she allows Tim to have his way just as she had done with her alcoholic mother. Ann decides she wants counseling help with her marriage and sees Steve, a counselor.

In their first session, Ann explains to Steve that she has told Tim she will no longer do his laundry, fix his meals, or have sex with him. Because Steve feels Ann is changing the contract without adequately having input from Tim, Steve asks her to bring Tim in so they can work on a new contract together.

Tim explains that every time he initiates sex, Ann cuts him off, and he feels resentful. "I still go to work. What if I just quit work?"

Ann replies, "He has had sex anytime he wants for twelve years, so if he feels resentful, that's just too bad."

When Steve asks Ann if she likes sex, she replies, "Yes, but I don't want to be dominated."

Steve explains that she can't throw the baby out with the bath water and her behavior is putting both Ann and Tim in a no-win situation. The three of them negotiate a new contract. The first week Ann will initiate sex, and the second week Tim will initiate. In addition, they both agree to split the chores.

The first week goes well with Ann initiating sex. The second week Tim tries, and Ann says no. Eventually, after four months of give and take in the area of sex and Tim meeting Ann's needs around the house, they become relaxed with a new contract that works for them.

1. What were Ann's beliefs *before* recovery?
    a. Tim has no goodwill toward me (which causes her to change the contract without negotiating).
    b. It's all my way or nothing.

2. What were Ann's changed beliefs *in* recovery?
    a. I believe Tim has goodwill toward me and does love me.
    b. I helped to set up the contract that has become unhealthy and overburdening, so I'm as much a part of the problem as Tim is.
    c. I have other options besides giving in.

3. What were Ann's dominant feelings *before* recovery?
    a. Domination and hurt
    b. Anger and fear

4. What were her changed feelings *in* recovery?
    a. Strength
    b. Cooperation

5. What were Ann's behavior patterns *before* recovery?
    a. Taking too much responsibility
    b. Yielding in sex when she didn't want to and then resenting Tim
    c. Cutting Tim off and not talking to him because of fear

6. What were her changed behavior patterns *in* recovery?
    a. Working through a contract that allowed both people to win
    b. Being willing to compromise, negotiate, and work toward resolve

#2 RESCUING GEORGE

Donna met George in high school and felt sorry for him. Nobody liked George, but Donna was such a giving, quiet, and congenial person that it was easy for her to get along with him. George drank in high school, but not around Donna. In college, George made a commitment to become a Christian. Donna nurtured George in the faith, but he seemed to be on guard and distant. George and Donna were married in their last year of college. Donna said, "George had been mistreated by so many people, especially his alcoholic dad, that I wanted to make him feel loved."

When George would get mad, Donna would quiet the children and try to make George comfortable. Over the years George began drinking more and more. Donna became tired of George's drinking and his temper tantrums. She went to several support meetings that encouraged her to stop taking responsibility for George's behavior. George couldn't understand why Donna was becoming cold and distant. He felt it was the fault of the groups she attended, so he attacked them and demanded she quit going. Donna didn't want to give up the meetings because she felt people finally understood her, and that brought her relief. So she told George she wouldn't quit the groups and asked if he would go to counseling to work out the relationship. Here's how their conversation developed:

George: What's wrong with our relationship is that you're going to that group and getting your head filled with nonsense. If you'd quit that group, we'd be fine.

Donna: I know you're angry with the group, but it's really my choice to change. The group is only helping me.

George: Those women just get together to bad-mouth their husbands. You do the same. I know you want out of this relationship—and you call yourself a Christian.

Donna: I know you're angry at me and that you don't want things to change. I can see this is hard on you, George. I'm changing, and I'm not willing to be yelled at anymore.

George: Fine! Then you're the one breaking up this marriage.

Donna: I'm not willing to continue with the way it was unless you get help for your anger and your drinking.

George: You don't care about me. You just want out of this relationship.

Donna: Don't tell me what I want. Do you want to work on this relationship or not? I do, and I'm willing to work to keep it.

1. What were Donna's beliefs *before* recovery?

2. What were her changed beliefs *in* recovery?

3. What were Donna's dominant feelings *before* recovery?

4. What were her changed feelings *in* recovery?

5. What were Donna's behavior patterns *before* recovery?

6. What were her changed behavior patterns *in* recovery?

7. How are you like Donna?

RECOVERY PROBERS

1. How do you get manipulated into doing something you don't want to do or accepting something you don't want?

2. What do you need to change to make the contract work? For example, "I'm willing to share financial responsibility only if you are willing to stay out of debt."

3. What part of the contract are you changing? Is the other person going to be left feeling cheated? How? How can you compensate by contributing in another way?

4. What are you not willing to do anymore? Where can you compromise? Do you have a clear conscience about the changes you're making?

5. What parts of the old relationship must die?

6. What will the new contract be like?

7. Do you need a mediator to help you change contracts?

8. How would you feel if your boss just lowered your wages without consulting you? What should your boss do if he or she had to lower them?

9. Is a one-sided change in a relationship contract ever appropriate? (Example: adultery)

RECOVERY GUIDE

God had a conditional contract with Israel, and his response to them was based on their commitment to the covenant or contract.

Read Deuteronomy 28:1–26.
1. What did God require of Israel?

2. What was God's part of the contract? Note how clearly he spelled out his part.

Read Genesis 2:15–17.
1. What were the conditions of the agreement?

2. What were the consequences of breaking the agreement?

Read Exodus 32:9–14.
1. How did Moses negotiate with God?

2. Why was God willing to change his mind?

Read Joshua 9.
1. Why did Israel honor the covenant with the Hivites, even though the Hivites manipulated them?

2. What are your basic contracts?

RECOVERY GOALS
1. What are your unspoken contracts?

2. In which relationships do you need to clarify what you are and aren't willing to do?

3. How will you attempt to do this? (Examples: discussion, letter, mediation)

4. If you quit certain behavior patterns, will others feel unloved or cheated? Which behavior patterns might influence these feelings?

5. What else could you do to reciprocate or make them feel loved? Commit these changes to God.

6. Work on negotiating a contract that is in need of a change. Write out what you want changed as well as what you think the other person in the relationship might want changed.

9. Breaking the Pattern: Intervention

RECOVERY FOCUS

- Recognize the dynamics of your destructive relational pattern.
- Determine your part in the unhealthy pattern.
- Find the appropriate helper to assist in an intervention.

RECOVERY INFORMATION

In some cases, setting boundaries and negotiating contracts will not be enough, and you may need to consider intervening in some way to break the destructive pattern. Interventions come in all forms. They can be as subtle as changes in behavior or attitude, or they can be a more structured confrontation—sometimes involving several people—that will bring a person to a point of seeking help.

Interventions are not magic. Once an intervention breaks a cycle, a person isn't guaranteed a "happily-ever-after" life. Follow-through is essential to keep the cycle broken, and even then, recovery doesn't always happen. Sometimes it is only after the second, third, or fourth intervention that the pattern is finally broken.

CODEPENDENCY CONFUSION

The confusion for Christians often comes from a perspective that feels interventions aren't loving, especially if the intervention involves a strong confrontation. But we need to remember, again, that we're not talking about normal behavior here; the destructive pattern is an unbalanced behavior that needs to be brought to wholeness. Doing that sometimes involves an escalation of confrontation, not unlike the pattern described in Matthew 18:15–17: "If your brother sins against you, go and show him his fault, just between the two of you. If he listens to you, you have won your brother over. But if he will not listen, take one or two others along, so that 'every matter may be established by the testimony of two or three witnesses.' If he refuses to listen to them, tell it to the church; and if he refuses to listen even to the church, treat him as you would a pagan or a tax collector." This pattern of church discipline is similar to what is used by addiction treatment centers today.

Breaking sinful or destructive cycles is loving and biblical. "So watch yourselves. If your brother sins, rebuke him, and if he repents, forgive him" (Luke 17:3). It may not be your natural instinct to rebuke or confront a person who sins; you, like many codependents, may be a pleaser or nurturer who minimizes sin and shortcomings, always forgiving and reconciling without the other person ever dealing with his or her issues.

Not all interventions must be the classic kind described in some of the recovery stories that follow. Some interventions can be handled just as effectively in a humorous way. Jack and Jill had established a destructive pattern of handling their anger. When Jack got angry, he yelled. Jill was afraid of his anger and reacted either by getting cold and distant or angry and "in-his-face." A counselor asked Jill to try an experiment, an intervention to break the pattern; the counselor explained that instead of opposing Jack's anger, she should join him in it as a way of calling attention to the effects of his behavior.

A week later, Jill had an opportunity to try the counselor's strategy. When Jack became frustrated over his lack of success on a project in the garage, he swore, picked up a box, and threw it. Jill usually would have given him a disapproving look, and the cycle would have begun. Instead, she picked up a box and threw it. Jack was caught off guard; he got angrier and threw another box. Jill picked up another box and threw it. After five minutes of both of them throwing boxes, they found themselves laughing together. A cycle was broken, bringing relief and bonding.

RECOVERY STORIES

#1 JUDY INTERVENES

Judy, an intelligent Christian, was married to an alcoholic and verbally abusive husband. She felt powerless about her interaction with her husband and often got depressed. "He gets angry when I don't do what he wants; then he drinks and destroys things in the house. I feel guilty half the time, as if it's my fault that he drinks. The rest of the time I feel angry because of his behavior. I'm on an emotional roller coaster. When I ask him if he's mad at me, he says no, but then he tells me how selfish I am."

Judy went to her pastor for counseling, but because she was embarrassed by Steve's drinking, she didn't tell the pastor about Steve's drunkenness and abuse. The pastor encouraged her to "be loving and win him by example."

After years of counseling, not much had improved. In fact, Steve's drinking increased. Judy felt trapped, as if something inside of her was dying. The pastor referred her to a professional counselor.

Judy worked hard in counseling and began to achieve some emotional independence. She said, "He doesn't make me feel guilty all the time anymore." About six months into counseling, she began to gain some control over her own life. She felt getting a part-time job would help, so she asked Steve what he thought about it. He got angry and said, "I don't care. Do whatever you want. You'll do what you want anyway!"

Judy didn't buy into the guilt and didn't react in her codependent fashion. Instead she said, "So it's okay with you if I take a part-time job?" Steve didn't say anything; he just walked out of the room. Judy got a part-time job. Steve insisted she quit counseling because he was sure she was having an affair with the counselor. Judy gave in and wasn't involved in any counseling for two years.

One night after drinking too much, Steve made a huge scene at a restaurant. Judy found herself embarrassed and making excuses for him. That night as she lay in bed, she decided that all her good exemplary behavior, her pleading, her covering up and nagging hadn't done any good and that she needed to do something that worked. She returned to the counselor she had seen two years earlier. Now she was stronger and ready to confront Steve's drinking.

The counselor suggested an intervention with an alcohol treatment center. Judy was willing to do anything at this point. As she began preparing for the intervention, members of her church told her it wasn't right for her to confront her husband. They believed she was too critical of Steve, and they wouldn't support an intervention. Judy felt all alone. She wasn't sure whether or not she was doing the right thing. She was tempted to return to the security of the status quo.

After wrestling in prayer, Judy decided to do the intervention. On a Sunday morning, a dozen family members, peers from work, and friends confronted Steve with his alcoholism and said they would no longer ignore his drinking. Steve fought everyone for three hours of emotional confrontation. Judy wanted to be loyal, but she also realized Steve had a choice in this marriage and that she needed to let him be responsible for his drinking. It took all her strength not to cave in. It was now up to God and Steve, and Judy found herself resting nervously in that thought. Steve decided on treatment and has maintained his sobriety.

Ten years later, Judy dropped by the counselor's office and left a note saying: "Steve has had ten years of sobriety and we are doing well. I can't tell you how much this has meant in my life. All those years of misery have now been replaced by good years. Although our marriage still has its occasional ups and downs, life is wonderful. Thanks again for all your help."

1. What were Judy's beliefs *before* recovery?
    a. The best way to deal with Steve's drinking is to cover up for him.
    b. If I change my behavior, Steve will stop drinking.
    c. Steve's already hostile toward God. I don't want to alienate him further. I'll try to win him with kindness.

2. What were her changed beliefs *in* recovery?
    a. Steve needs to take responsibility for his drinking.
    b. I can't change him, but he can change if he's willing to pay a price.
    c. I need help from other people to confront Steve with the consequences of his behavior.

3. What were Judy's dominant feelings *before* recovery?
    a. Frustration and anger
    b. Guilt and embarrassment
    c. Desperation and helplessness

4. What were her changed feelings *in* recovery?
    a. Confidence in God's ability to help Steve face his problems
    b. Determination to confront Steve
    c. Openness to receiving help from others

5. What were Judy's behavior patterns *before* recovery?
    a. Taking too much responsibility
    b. Trying to avoid Steve's angry outbursts
    c. Covering up for Steve's alcoholism

6. What were her changed behavior patterns *in* recovery?

78 CODEPENDENCY CONFUSION

    a. Making Steve responsible for his own problems
    b. Taking steps to intervene
    c. Involving others in the process of intervention

#2 JOE GETS A JOB

For several years Pat had financially supported her husband. She had a great career, and he had a series of part-time jobs. They had talked about starting a family, but Joe made no moves toward a full-time job. Pat found she was taking more and more responsibility in the relationship as the years rolled on. When she confronted Joe, he accused her of being selfish and unchristian. She felt guilty and quieted her complaints.

Pat came to the end of her rope and considered divorcing Joe. She even fantasized about Joe dying in a car accident.

Finally she decided to go to her pastor for help. He listened, saw the seriousness of her situation, and called Joe into the office. The pastor told Joe he needed to get a job that could support his family. He asked Joe if this was his intention, and Joe said yes. The pastor then asked Pat what she heard. She said that Joe had been promising to get a full-time job for years but hadn't done anything about it. The pastor set up a time limit in which Joe was to get a full-time job. The pastor helped Joe with follow-through and held him accountable.

Joe found a job two weeks before the limit was up, and Pat was able to work with Joe on the issue of starting a family. This intervention broke a pattern in which Joe's intentions were great but his passive resistance sabotaged any movement out of the "stuckness" in his relationship with Pat.

1. What were Pat's beliefs *before* recovery?

2. What were her changed beliefs *in* recovery?

3. What were Pat's dominant feelings *before* recovery?

4. What were her changed feelings *in* recovery?

5. What were Pat's behavior patterns *before* recovery?

6. What were her changed behavior patterns *in* recovery?

6. How are you like Pat?

RECOVERY PROBERS

1. In what relationships might you want to consider an intervention?

2. What types of interventions will you need to make?

3. What is the level of intensity in your relationship?

4. Do you need help in doing an intervention?

Types of Interventions

Prayer intervention. Prayer is the first line of intervention. Enlist other people in praying for you, but show respect for the other person by not betraying confidences in your prayer requests.

Legal intervention. Physical abuse or sexual abuse calls for legal intervention. You may need help from the police or an agency like Child and Family Services.

Church-related intervention. If the person is consistently violating a scriptural imperative and has already been confronted individually, the church can be brought in.

Treatment-center intervention. Treatment centers are effective in interventions against addictions, such as alcohol, drugs, sex, food, or gambling.

Counseling intervention. When relationships consistently reach impasses and neither person has skills to work through them, you may need to get counseling help. A psychologist or psychiatrist also needs to be brought in if the person suffers from mood disorders, character disorders, or thought disorders.

Personal intervention. A personal intervention is a situation in which you are willing to make changes and work on your own issues, regardless of what the other person does or doesn't do.

RECOVERY GUIDE

Read 1 Corinthians 5:1–13.

The church at Corinth had many believers who were struggling or active in their sins. Paul didn't say that everyone who was active needed to be cast out of the church; in fact, the Corinthians were accepted almost in spite of their condition. However, one man had been sleeping with his father's wife, and this was a horrible sin to overlook. Because the Corinthians were guilty of minimizing this offense, Paul exhorted them to make an issue of this sin rather than let it go.

1. Is it biblical to judge or evaluate another person's life? How does this passage give us that responsibility (vv. 12–13)?

2. If we know a Christian persists in practicing something that is wrong, what intervention is suggested here (vv. 7–11)?

Read 2 Timothy 2:24–26.

1. How is this intervention different from that described in 1 Corinthians 5?

2. Who is responsible to change the person who is wrong?

Read Romans 12:17–21.

1. How is this intervention, which deals with personal suffering from evil, different from the interventions described in other passages?

2. Why would this intervention emphasize letting go rather than confronting?

RECOVERY GOALS

1. In what relationships should you consider doing an intervention?

2. What are your motives in choosing to intervene?

3. When and where would you do the intervention?

4. What type of intervention would you do?

5. Whose help would you enlist?

6. What would prevent you from following through with an intervention?

7. What do you plan to do about it?

8. Write out a step-by-step plan explaining what you need to do to make the intervention happen. Pray about every step of the plan.

10. Finding Love in Healthy Ways

RECOVERY FOCUS

- Recognize manipulation and pursuit as unhealthy ways of finding love.
- Find acceptance and security in your relationship with God.
- Learn to feel confident even when others are not available to you.

RECOVERY INFORMATION

If you are like many codependents, you feel desperate when you sense you are cut off—either emotionally or physically—from a person. You may find that you will do anything in order to avoid rejection or abandonment.

LOOK IN THE MIRROR

Read the following characteristics and check those that describe you:

- ☐ I do things that violate my conscience in order to stay connected.
- ☐ I whine or make sarcastic remarks about not having my needs met. (Example: "I can't remember the last time you brought me flowers.")
- ☐ I cry and cling to other people, smothering or engulfing them.
- ☐ I withdraw, promising myself never again to expect anything.
- ☐ I know I am violating other people's physical and emotional boundaries, but I can't stop myself.
- ☐ I beg and plead with them to love me.

You may believe that if someone doesn't take care of you, you will die. As a result, you pursue a physical connection—a show of affection, touch, or sex—and feel wonderful when the connection is made. Or you may pursue an emotional connection: a compliment, attention, a warm greeting, or a good engaging fight. You may know in your head that pursuing or manipulating other people isn't healthy, but you feel powerless to make any change.

The goal of recovery in this issue is to find healthy ways of meeting your needs for love, security, and value. This first step is recognizing that your present patterns are unhealthy. That is not to say that your *needs* are unhealthy—quite the contrary. We all need to find love, value, and security. The question is, Where do you get those needs met?

The second step is to realize that your needs must first be met through your relationship with God. Before you dismiss this suggestion as unrealistic and pious, think about it carefully. Remember what we said in chapter 1: "When we depend on circumstances or relationships to give us security, self-esteem, or identity, we are disappointed. People and circumstances let us down. . . . We should depend, first of all, on God for our value, self-esteem, and security." As you learn to find your worth and love in your Father God, your fear of abandonment will subside, and you will find yourself less and less desperate to manipulate people to love you.

A third step is to broaden your emotional support by building healthy relationships with family and friends. Sharing personal interests or simple pleasures with other people will help you lose your sense of insecurity in your codependent relationships.

CODEPENDENCY CONFUSION

Maybe the most confusing aspect for Christian codependents in this chapter involves expectations. Is it wrong to believe that your family and friends will love you the way you need to be loved? Is it wrong to pursue that expectation in faith and confidence? Surely God is big enough and powerful enough to create good relationships.

These assumptions may be true, but they also may be expectations that just aren't realistic. It is difficult to know how God works, even though we know his heart. However, pursuers who are becoming desperate lose their confidence, dignity, and self-esteem and become codependents who are really passive, dependent victims.

RECOVERY STORIES
#1 IVY AND SECURITY

Many years ago a woman named Security had a son. He was a beautiful baby, and everyone commented on how handsome he was. Security named him Ivy and loved him very much. In fact, all the people of the village loved Ivy and enjoyed playing with him. He was a responsive child and had a smile that lit up a room.

One day while Ivy was playing outside, Security came out and asked him to do something. Ivy refused and Security said, "I'll leave you if you aren't good." Ivy didn't take her seriously and went on playing. A little later he came in the house, and his mother was gone. Ivy began to panic. He felt sick to his stomach and was overwhelmed. He thought for sure he had lost Security.

He yelled out, "I'll do anything! Please don't leave me!" Ivy was afraid and began crying and pleading out loud, "I'll be good! I promise! Just come back, ple-e-ease!"

Suddenly a door opened, and Security walked in. Ivy ran and embraced her, but she was cold and angry. Ivy didn't care; at least she was back. Ivy would hardly leave Security after that day.

Security demanded unconditional loyalty from Ivy. He wasn't allowed to question her, even if he felt something was really wrong in the relationship. Ivy began to feel mixed up inside. His responsiveness and his bright smile began to fade.

One day as Ivy was walking through town, a team of horses broke loose and started running down the main street. Ivy didn't see the horses running at him. Just at the moment it looked as if Ivy would be stomped to death, a boy ran out of the crowd and pushed Ivy to safety. However, the boy was killed in attempting to save Ivy's life. An old man knelt over the trampled body of the boy. A gentle tear streaked his face. He was the boy's father.

A week later, Ivy went to visit the old man, expecting to meet with bitterness and resentment. Instead, what he found was a strong man who could cry and be tender. Ivy began to spend many afternoons with the old man. They developed a relationship, and Ivy began to get back the spark in his eyes. He found he didn't have to deny his feelings and thoughts around the old man, even though the man didn't always approve of them or agree with him. This new loyalty contained freedom and seemed to supply strength and confidence to Ivy.

However, this relationship was a threat to Security, and she intended to put a stop to it. One day she came to Ivy and said, "Ivy, you have to stop seeing that old man. He is bad, and I won't stand for your being with him anymore." Ivy was confused. He tried to talk to his mother, but she wouldn't reason with him and began to distance herself. An old, terrifying feeling started to come over Ivy, and he felt sick.

Ivy went to visit the old man and told him about losing Security, his mother, and how he felt. After he finished, the old man replied, "Sometimes when you let go, you don't lose but gain."

Ivy's reply was, "But I'm so afraid."

The old man said, very gently, "Ivy, you can trust me. I ask you to think about what I have said." Somehow as Ivy embraced those words, he felt free. This was a new beginning for Ivy.

1. **What were Ivy's beliefs *before* recovery?**
   a. I can't be myself and be loyal to my mother. I can't think and feel on my own without threat of losing the relationship.
   b. I wouldn't have personal security, confidence, or well-being without my mother's loyalty and approval.
   c. I can't endure those horrible and desperate feelings of separation.

2. **What were his changed beliefs *in* recovery?**
   a. Loyalty means I'm committed not only to the relationship and the other person but also to myself.
   b. With God's help, I can survive without the approval and loyalty of others.
   c. Suffering often seems to weaken us, but in the long run, it strengthens us.

3. **What were Ivy's dominant feelings *before* recovery?**
   a. Panic over fear of abandonment
   b. Desperation and self-doubt
   c. Loneliness, isolation, and emptiness

4. **What were his changed feelings *in* recovery?**
   a. Anxiety mixed with confidence and hope
   b. Security through having direction
   c. A sense of belonging; sometimes alone but not lonely

5. **What were Ivy's behavior patterns *before* recovery?**
   a. Paralyzed in thought, feelings, and desires
   b. Clinging and childish behavior patterns, pleading, begging, and clutching

c. Yielding, motivated by fear

6. **What were his changed behavior patterns *in* recovery?**
   a. Forming a new, healthy alliance
   b. Breaking an unconditional loyalty that kept him from thinking and dealing with his feelings and desires
   c. Becoming more assertive

#2 SARAH'S DAD

Sarah loved her father very much but also feared his disapproval. Even though Sarah had a family, she spent lots of time with her dad. She went to him anytime he wanted to see her. Sarah's dad punished her with silence for weeks if she didn't please him.

This relationship caused lots of friction in Sarah's marriage. In fact, her husband complained that "She's married to him, not me. If her dad calls, she jumps and runs to him." Eventually Sarah's marriage collapsed.

Sarah came to counseling because she was depressed and anxious. Much of her anxiety was connected to her relationship with her father and her divorce. The counselor helped Sarah devise a strategy for resisting her father's manipulation.

When her father called Sarah and asked if she would take him shopping, she simply said no; she had an after-school commitment with her daughter. He had his own car, and Sarah knew he could do the errand by himself if he wanted to.

He immediately began his attack. "You don't love me. After all I've done for you, and you can't take me to the store."

Sarah very directly said, "No, Dad, I'm not going to give you a ride today. If you want to go tomorrow, give me a call."

Usually Sarah's dad wouldn't talk to her for weeks until Sarah broke and asked him to forgive her. This time Sarah was coached not to placate her father but also not to be afraid or withdraw from him. She would have been anxious, but she kept herself busy instead. She took walks, prayed, and talked to other people.

Sarah called her dad two days later, but he hung up on her after picking a fight. Sarah felt afraid and was tempted to fall back into her old patterns. She fought her impulse to call him and apologize. However, she maintained her resolve. She held off until her dad began to talk to her again. In fact, she felt her father's silence as a relief. "I can live without his approval," she boasted to her counselor. "I've always needed to be in his good graces, but now I feel so much freer. I don't feel guilty, abandoned, or anxious."

1. What were Sarah's beliefs *before* recovery?

2. What were her changed beliefs *in* recovery?

3. What were Sarah's dominant feelings *before* recovery?

4. What were her changed feelings *in* recovery?

5. What were Sarah's behavior patterns *before* recovery?

6. What were her changed behavior patterns *in* recovery?

7. How are you like Sarah?

RECOVERY PROBERS

1. What can you do to take care of your needs for love and emotional security instead of expecting other people to meet them?

2. What is the worst thing that can happen if your family member, friend, or co-worker doesn't approve of you?

3. If you are rejected, will you die? How?

4. Does it help to deny your needs and expectations? Why or why not?

5. What is unconditional loyalty? How does it help cover up family secrets? How does it keep you from getting your needs met?

6. How can you get through your anxious feelings of abandonment and rejection? What can you do to feel better when you are cut off?

RECOVERY GUIDE

God's words to Israel declare how he values and loves you: "I have called you by name; you are mine. . . . You are precious to me and honored, and I love you. . . . I have made [you] for my glory; I created [you]" (Isa. 43:1–7 TLB).

1. How do these words make you feel?

2. Memorize these words, saying them aloud when you feel desperate and abandoned.

Read Joshua 1:5.

1. What is the promise and how does it relate to abandonment and Joshua's insecurity?

2. When you feel alone, visualize God's presence with you wherever you are—in the car, at home alone, in church, with your family.

FINDING LOVE IN HEALTHY WAYS 89

Read Psalm 118:5-9.

1. What does it mean for you specifically to "take refuge" in the Lord?

2. What are some practical things you can do with God and yourself to overcome your anxiety?

RECOVERY GOALS

1. Who are you afraid will cut you off?

2. How do you pursue them? Which of your behavior patterns are inappropriate?

3. When will you be willing to discontinue pursuing them and stop all inappropriate behavior patterns? (When you feel insecure, do something to make yourself feel better rather than trying to get someone else to make you feel better.)

4. How will you do this? How will you take care of your fear of abandonment?

5. What would prevent you from taking care of yourself? How can you keep that from happening?

LEADER'S GUIDE

WORKING WITH CODEPENDENTS

Because most codependents see themselves as victims, you will be hearing a lot about the perpetrator, the person who hurts, abuses, frustrates, or scares the codependent. Your job will be to help the group provide relief, support, and stability to the codependent without judging and turning against the perpetrator. Try to maintain neutrality and balance, not allowing yourself to see the perpetrator as the "bad guy," even though you may hear evil things the perpetrator does.

Working with codependents can be seductive for group leaders and members. Many codependents' relationships seem to be so traumatic that any available support is like a glass of cold water to a person walking in the desert. The person or group who fills this role of providing support, relief from anxiety, and stability needs to be careful. It's often easy to play into the codependents' needs and weaknesses and further the codependency rather than help to break it.

Don't be surprised if codependents resist any direction you may give them in moving toward recovery and personal responsibility. Some codependents will accept only support; they see caregiving as love and suggestions for change as rejection. Don't be afraid to confront this assumption, either in the group as a whole or in one or two people who refuse to take personal responsibility. Do it gently, but do it. Growth takes time, and a mature leader shows discernment in knowing when to be patient and when to push a bit. Again, the key dynamic is balance: give enough support so that the codependent is enabled to grow but not so much support that the codependent becomes dependent on the group in unhealthy ways.

Be careful not to allow yourself or the support group to become a substitute for codependents' primary relationships. Some codependents establish a stronger alliance with their support group or leader than they have with their spouse. This can undermine not only the marriage but also codependents' recovery process.

Some groups make a huge difference in the codependent's life. However, for the unhealthy relationship to gain balance, the family members or other people in the codependent's relationship must do their work too. If they wish to work through this workbook or attend a group or go to counseling, that would be very helpful.

The more intense the situation, the more difficult it is to help the codependent. Don't hesitate to refer group members to trained pastors, counselors, or treatment centers. If you are unsure about a group member, get permission and talk to someone who would be knowledgeable.

The recovery process takes time and patience. Remember to entrust each of the group members to God's care. You are not ultimately responsible for any person's recovery. You can pray, encourage, support, challenge, and point the person in the right direction. The rest is up to the codependent and God.

If you have doubts about your qualifications to lead a codependency support group, see the "Qualifications for Codependency Support-Group Leader" section of this leader's guide.

PURPOSE OF GROUP

1. To give hope
2. To give information
3. To break codependents' isolation and pain
4. To help codependents heal and grow
5. To point codependents to God for help
6. To help codependents develop better relational skills

GROUP FORMAT

Depending on the length of time the group will meet, you can use a variety of formats. The shorter format may be more realistic for groups that meet as part of a church's Christian-education program, which may be organizied in semesters. If possible, take a full year; twelve months provides people a better pace in which to assimilate the material into their lives. Whether you choose a three-month group or a one-year group, we recommend that the group size be the same: 8–12 members.

Opening Sessions

1. Define the purpose of the group.
2. Read together the Group Ground Rules, found on the following pages.
3. Have each person take 10–15 minutes to give his or her personal background and tell his or her story.
4. Define your expectations of attendance and workbook involvement. Get clear commitments from group members.

Workbook Sessions
1. Open with prayer.
2. Share victories, especially those related to previous chapters. Encourage people to share goals they have met.
3. Discuss the various sections of the week's chapter.
4. Share current struggles. Allow people time to work on struggles.
5. Close with prayer.

Closing Sessions
1. Focus on what has been gained by reflecting on victories.
2. Talk about what relationships have been meaningful.
3. Make a commitment to have a reunion in three months.

GROUP GROUND RULES
1. All conversations in the group are confidential and may not be shared with anyone outside the group. If permission is asked and everyone is comfortable, an exception can be made. Protection leading to trust building is a goal of this group.
2. Members aren't responsible for other members; group members are not responsible for giving advice, excusing other people's actions, or fixing hurting people. Group members may share experience from their point of view if information is wanted.
3. Listen without interrupting. Each person's story and experience is valuable. Each group member is valuable.
4. Avoid using "shoulds" or "oughts" in the group, either for yourself or others.
5. If a group member becomes anxious about the group experience, talk about it in the group. If a group member wants to quit the group over fearful feelings or resentment, talk about it in the group. Check whether the person is seeing things realistically, helping him or her to see if the fear is warranted or just a part of the recovery process.
6. Stay on the goals and purposes of the group and keep conversations directed.

GROUP PROCESS
Groups form in stages. The initial stage is one of bonding, a stage in which group members share about themselves and find out if the group is safe. The leader's role is to facilitate safety and openness.

Leaders need to work toward giving everyone the opportunity to share. Be careful not to allow group members to try to rescue each other.

In later stages, the group members will jockey for positions. Don't be surprised if group members challenge your leadership and some members re-create in the group the dysfunctional behavior that made them codependent in the first place. Your role is to avoid thinking like a victim and to move the group and its members toward personal responsibility, godliness, and healthy thinking. This gives opportunity for real dialogue between group members and for teaching of new skills.

In the last stages, the group needs to learn to let go and say goodbye in a healthy way. Help the group to focus on what they have learned and how they have grown. Help group members reflect on their victories and express their joy from relationships. Your role will be one of helping members not to rationalize but to face their feelings of loss and to express tenderness to each other.

REFERRALS

People who attend a group like this often have problems that are more serious than a codependency support group can handle. Remember that codependents are rescuers who overestimate their abilities to help people. If group members have chemical dependencies, sexual addictions, mental illnesses, or suffer from physical or sexual abuse, refer them to the appropriate professionals. (See chapter 9, "Breaking the Pattern: Intervention" for information on the types of referrals that may be appropriate.) If a group member is already in counseling, this group will be an effective adjunct to that individual therapy. Most competent counselors will be happy to have their clients in a support group.

SUGGESTED QUALIFICATIONS FOR GROUP LEADERS

For maximum effectiveness, leaders will have
1. attended a secular CODA (Codependents Anonymous) meeting or ALANON (for family members of alcoholics) meeting for a year or more.
2. been Christians for several years and will have a basic knowledge of the Bible and Christian doctrines. Leaders will have a dynamic

relationship to Christ and a commitment to pray daily for their group members.
3. achieved and maintained some stability in their codependent or dysfunctional relationships.
4. experience in facilitating a group. If possible, leaders will first serve as co-leaders of a group before having primary leadership responsibilities.
5. experience teaching and practicing basic communication skills, such as "using 'I messages,'" "reflective listening," "taking ownership," "request making," and the like.
6. read books about codependence and will have worked through personal issues in these books.
7. accountability to the leaders of the facility in which the support group meets. For instance, if the group meets in a church and is sanctioned by the church, support-group leaders will be accountable to the church's leadership.

SUGGESTED READINGS

If you found this Recovery Discovery workbook helpful, you may also find help from the following books:

Berry, Carmen Renee. *When Helping You Is Hurting Me: Escaping the Messiah Trap.* San Francisco: Harper & Row, 1988.

Ells, Alfred. *One-Way Relationships.* Nashville: Nelson, 1990.

Hemfelt, Robert; Minirth, Frank; and Meier, Paul. *Love Is a Choice: Recovery for Codependent Relationships.* Nashville: Nelson, 1989.

Hemfelt, Robert and Warren, Paul. *Kids Who Carry Our Pain: Breaking the Cycle of Codependency for the Next Generation.* Nashville: Nelson, 1990.

Rinck, Margaret J. *Can Christians Love Too Much? Breaking the Cycle of Codependency.* Grand Rapids: Zondervan, 1989.

Silvious, Jan. *Please Don't Say You Need Me: Biblical Answers for Codependency.* Grand Rapids: Zondervan, 1989.

Springle, Pat. *Rapha's 12-Step Program for Overcoming Codependency.* Waco, Tex.: Rapha and Word, 1990.